# GREAT PURSUITS

CHASING WHAT MATTERS MOST IN LIFE

BAYLESS CONLEY

Answers Press
© 2020 by Bayless Conley
First Printing 2020

Answers with Bayless Conley
PO Box 417
Los Alamitos, CA 90720

Visit our website at www.BaylessConley.tv.

ISBN-13: 978-0-9981178-1-2
ISBN-10: 0-9981178-1-1

All Scripture quotations, unless otherwise indicated, are taken from the New King James Version, copyright © 1982 by Thomas Nelson. Used by permission. All rights reserved.

Scripture quotations marked (AMPC) are taken from the Amplified® Bible (AMPC), Copyright © 1954, 1958, 1962, 1964, 1965, 1987 by The Lockman Foundation (www.Lockman.org). Used by permission.

Scripture quotations marked (ERV) are taken from the HOLY BIBLE: EASY-TO-READ VERSION © 2014 by Bible League International. Used by permission.

Scripture quotations marked (MSG) are taken from *THE MESSAGE,* copyright © 1993, 1994, 1995, 1996, 2000, 2001, 2002 by Eugene H. Peterson. Used by permission of NavPress. All rights reserved. Represented by Tyndale House Publishers, Inc.

Scripture quotations marked (NLT) are taken from the Holy Bible, New Living Translation, copyright © 1996, 2004, 2007, 2013, 2015 by Tyndale House Foundation. Used by permission of Tyndale House Publishers, Inc., Carol Stream, Illinois 60188. All rights reserved.

Scripture quotations marked (NIV) are taken from the Holy Bible, New International Version®, NIV® Copyright © 1973, 1978, 1984, 2011 by Biblica, Inc.® Used by permission. All rights reserved worldwide.

Scripture quotations marked (TLB) are taken from The Living Bible, copyright © 1971. Used by permission of Tyndale House Publishers, Inc., Carol Stream, Illinois 60188. All rights reserved.

All rights reserved. No part of this publication may be reproduced, stored in a retrieval system, or transmitted, in any form or by any means—electronic, mechanical, photocopying, recording, or otherwise—without prior written permission from the author.

*Printed in United States of America.*

# CONTENTS

| | | |
|---|---|---:|
| | *Introduction* | 1 |
| 1. | The Pursuit of Peace | 3 |
| 2. | The Pursuit of the Knowledge of the Lord | 21 |
| 3. | The Pursuit of Hospitality | 33 |
| 4. | The Pursuit of What Is Good | 41 |
| 5. | The Pursuit of Love | 49 |
| 6. | The Pursuit of Righteousness and Godliness | 61 |
| 7. | The Pursuit of Faith and Love | 77 |
| 8. | The Pursuit of Patience and Gentleness | 91 |
| 9. | Pursuing Purpose | 109 |
| 10. | Pursuing Lost Things | 129 |
| | *Postscript* | 149 |

# INTRODUCTION

It was that class again—the one where the students got to teach. Another hour of listening to what were, for the most part, very boring and generally highly plagiarized sermons. We were in Bible school and this was definitely **not** my favorite course, at least not until that day.

The first student gave his fifteen-minute sermonette while his classmates politely listened and the instructor scribbled notes as he critiqued the effort. When the second student got up to fill the next fifteen-minute slot, my whole universe turned sideways.

*She's cute. How is it that I've never noticed her before?* I thought to myself. I immediately planned to ambush her in the hallway once we were dismissed.

"That was good," I told her when I caught up to her as she made her way to her next class. After introductions and a little small talk, I got to it. "I'd like to take you to lunch sometime," I said. "I'll pray about it," she answered flatly. And she was gone. A few weeks later she got back to me. "You asked me to go to lunch with you. The answer is no."

If you haven't guessed it yet, that cute girl is now my wife, Janet. I gave it some time, but decided she was worth pursuing. I would ask her one more time. If I got a no again, I would move on. The second time I asked her out, she didn't say she needed to pray. She just said yes. Eight months later we were married.

I have never regretted my pursuit of Janet. We married in 1982 and next to accepting Christ, sharing my life with her has been the best decision that I have ever made.

In Scripture we are told very clearly to pursue certain things—first, because they are important, and second, because without an active pursuit, we will never experience them in our lives. These are blessings from God that will not automatically come to you **unless** you take action to pursue them just like He intended.

# 1

# THE PURSUIT OF PEACE

He who would love life and see good days, let him refrain his tongue from evil, and his lips from speaking deceit. Let him turn away from evil and do good; **let him seek peace and pursue it**.

1 Peter 3:10–11 (emphasis mine)

Peter quotes here from Psalm 34. In its original setting, it deals more with seeking peace with and from God. As it is used here in 1 Peter, the primary focus is seeking peace between men—both are essential. You can never truly have the highest peace with men without first experiencing peace with God.

## Peace with God

The quote found in Psalm 34:12–14 is prefaced with statements like: "I sought the Lord and He heard me and delivered me from all my fears" (v. 4), and "Oh, taste and see that the Lord is good; blessed is the man who trusts in Him" (v. 8), as well as "Come, you children, listen to me; I will teach you the fear of the Lord" (v. 11). The emphasis is clearly on having peace with God.

The unsaved world lives in opposition to God. But because Christ reconciled us to God while we were His enemies (Romans 5:10), we now have "peace with God through our Lord Jesus Christ" (Romans 5:1)!

Peace with God only comes as we surrender our lives to Him and accept—by faith—His glorious gift of salvation. It is not achieved or merited through our good works, personal sacrifice, or some spiritual journey or practice. He "made peace [for us] through the blood of His cross" (Colossians 1:20).

## The Peace of God

Once you've entered into peace with God, you can **experience** the peace of God in your daily life. It is a supernatural peace that defies human reasoning. It guards the heart and mind of the believer even in the most difficult storms of life. It comes to you as you unburden your heart before Him in prayer.

Philippians 4:6–7 gives us both a command and a promise: "Be anxious for nothing, but in everything by prayer and supplication, with thanksgiving, let your requests be made known to God; and the peace of God, which surpasses all understanding, will guard your hearts and minds through Christ Jesus."

In the simplest of terms, we are told to not worry about anything but to pray about everything. And once we make our request known, we are promised the peace of God. These verses don't promise that God will answer our requests (though that is implied and clearly taught elsewhere). But they do make an astonishing promise: talk to God about your problem, make your request known, and He will give you a peace that surpasses human understanding!

As human beings, we can only handle so much pressure. If there is no release of the built-up pressure due to the difficulties of life, eventually there will be some sort of an eruption or breakdown. It may erupt into marriage problems, mental health issues, outbursts of anger, broken health, or a myriad of other harmful issues. These can be avoided because God has given us the ultimate recipe for stress relief—prayer.

Years ago, I had come to the end of my rope. I had made the mistake of taking the word of a man who was doing some expensive construction work for me. He came highly recommended by a close friend and attended the same church that I did. To my dismay, this individual proved to be less than trustworthy, and the work that I had him do on a handshake turned out to be a huge mistake on my part. The cost suddenly doubled at the last minute and I found myself in a terrible predicament.

I didn't have the funds to pay him to finish the work, which created several other major problems for my family. I went into a tailspin. A deep depression settled over me and I saw no way out of the dilemma. My wife realized what a bad place I was in when I stopped responding to her. For a couple of days, I didn't communicate at all.

After a few days of having my brain feel like it would explode, I went outside and sat down on the curb in front of our house and said, "God, what am I going to do?" Immediately, I felt the Holy Spirit say to my heart, "Why don't you do what you preach to everyone else?" That is not what I wanted to hear. But I knew it was right.

I began to pray and pour out my heart to God. I talked to Him about the situation and asked for His help. An amazing thing happened. The circumstance didn't change, but I did. The burden lifted from me. My joy returned and an unexplainable peace flooded over me. I lifted my hands and began to shout in praise, walking back and forth in the street in front of my house. I'm sure some of the neighbors thought I had lost my mind, but I didn't care. I had peace and an assurance in my heart that things would work out. I had put things into the hands of my heavenly Father.

Within a week a miracle happened. All the necessary funds came in from a totally unexpected source. It was good to get out of the storm, but the lesson I had learned about the peace of God was beyond any price.

Whatever you're facing right now has not taken God by surprise. Why not take the time—right now—before you read any further and have a conversation with God. Let your requests be made known to Him. Unburden your heart and ask for His help. He will give you a peace that will guard your heart and mind, and you will find that He is a very present help in trouble.

## Peace with People

Where King David, in Psalm 34, had the emphasis on pursuing peace with and from God, Peter places the emphasis on **pursuing peace with people.** The surrounding verses in 1 Peter 3 make that clear. Verses 1–7 deal with husband-wife relationships, and then in verses 8–9, he says, "Finally, all of you be of one mind, having compassion for one another; love as brothers, be tenderhearted, be courteous; not returning evil for evil or reviling for reviling, but on the contrary blessing, knowing that you were called to this, that you may inherit a blessing." Then he follows up the exhortation to pursue peace with more insights and instructions concerning dealing with people that would try and harm, threaten, or trouble you as a believer in Christ (vv. 13–17).

Hebrews 12:14 reaffirms Peter's emphasis on the pursuit of peace. There, it plainly commands believers to "pursue peace with all people." *All people* includes your neighbor that's acting like a jerk. It includes your co-workers, your family, your brothers and your sisters in the Church, and the unsaved people in your community. *All people* means **all** people.

Romans 14:19 says, "Therefore let us pursue the things which make for peace and the things by which one may edify another." There are **things** we can do that will bring peace and **things** that we can do to edify, or build up, others. In fact, the things that build up generally bring peace, while the things that tear down generally shatter peace.

So what are those **things** that invite peace between people?

## Things That Make for Peace

# PRAYER

A good starting place when it comes to pursuing peace with people is prayer. In fact, the statement directly following the words, "Seek peace and pursue it," in Psalm 34:14 is, "The eyes of the Lord are on the righteous, and His ears are open to their cry" (v. 15). That is a direct reference to prayer.

Prayer changes things. Prayer brings the influence of God's Spirit to bear on situations and people's hearts. Sometimes things radically and suddenly shift once you begin to pray. The breakthroughs in relationships with people can be startling because they happen so quickly. And we all love it when that happens. Things turn from sour to sweet, an enemy becomes an ally, and a difficult person softens and perhaps even apologizes for his or her behavior or obstinacy.

But most of the time prayer initiates a process. A process where God **may** work a change in the person you're praying for, but where He **definitely** works a change in you. This is especially true when we begin to pray for someone that we don't have a healthy relationship with. In prayer, God will begin to change your heart and attitude. God may certainly do something in the person's heart for whom you pray, but we cannot control that. All you can do is cooperate with the work He is trying to do in you.

Christ's first teaching on prayer is found in Matthew 5:44 where He says, "But I say to you, love your enemies, bless those who curse you, do good to those who hate you, and pray for those who spitefully use you and persecute you."

It is obvious that we need the Holy Spirit's help to love our enemies, and from our hearts, to bless and do good to those who curse, harm, and hate us. And the way you invite the Holy Spirit to come and do His work in you is through honest, heartfelt prayer.

## God Opened My Eyes

Back in the early days of my pastoring, I foolishly gave a significant leadership role to an elderly man in our church. He had been a Christian longer than I had been alive and had much experience with churches. Sadly, I came to find out that much of that "experience" had to do with causing trouble in the previous churches he had been a part of. It proved no different with us.

He had very effectively sowed some seeds of dissension among our leadership team to the point where some previously healthy relationships had become quite strained. Eventually, several of our key leaders came to me and shared what this person had told them and how it had impacted their view of me. Each one of them also shared how the Holy Spirit had shown them the truth of the matter, and they had come to apologize to me and to say that they were no longer willing to listen to this man.

I immediately arranged a lunch with this older gentleman to get to the bottom of things and hopefully get them worked out. It proved fruitless. All through that lunch, I felt like I would have had a better time trying to get a fence post to see reason. He denied any wrongdoing and implied that God was going to judge me. The only positive thing that came of it was that he voluntarily stepped away from his leadership role in the church. He made it seem, however, that he was doing so because he didn't want to be too close to me when God's lightning struck me down.

The trouble he caused had harmed several important relationships, slowed the progress of the church, and even affected my health, but I was about to learn an unexpected lesson.

Several weeks later, as I was spending some alone time with God in my office, this man came to my heart and I began to pray for him. A very unexpected thing happened. The only way that I can explain it is to say that God opened my eyes. As I prayed, I suddenly saw this man from God's point of view. I was given a direct look into his heart. What I saw astounded me. I realized that he had believed all along that he was doing the right thing. He had been deceived, but he didn't know it. He actually thought he had been right in the things he had done and said. I never dreamed that he was without malice toward me.

That encounter with God in prayer changed me. I realized that God alone sees to the core of people's hearts. Though I would not trust that man with another leadership role, I realized he was not my enemy. Where previously there had been hurt and extreme anxiety for me, there was peace. In fact, from that time on I treated that man with respect and kindness.

Soon after, he left the church. If I saw him today, I could shake his hand or hug his neck without any ill feelings. Through prayer I had found peace from God. Peace in my soul and peace with a man that I formerly looked at as a foe.

## COMMUNICATION

Most of the time, if you are going to have peace with someone where there are differences of opinion or perception—or where hostility has existed—you will have to talk with them. Have some "peace talks," which means you will need to do as much listening as you do talking.

Proverbs 18:19 says, "A brother offended is harder to win than a strong city, and contentions are like the bars of a castle." That means that making peace will take much effort and thoughtful planning. A strong city or a fortified castle is not won by the thoughtless or by the impatient. And neither is an offended brother.

Those that don't take the time or effort to pursue a damaged relationship generally do not do so for one of two reasons. The first reason is because they don't value the relationship. It just isn't important enough to them to put in the necessary effort to bring peace. If you can identify with this, keep in mind that **you may need to someday walk across the bridge you allow to burn down.** The second reason, which is more likely, is they don't know how to pursue peace within a broken relationship. Maybe your life experience has not taught you how or you've never been given the necessary tools to reconcile or to make peace. If so, that's okay. We've all been shaped by our past, but Christ is here in your present and He can empower you to pursue peace.

### *Being Right Isn't the Goal—Peace Is*

As we have already covered, it starts with prayer. Talk to God about yourself and about the person you are at odds with, **and then talk to the person.** And when you do speak with them, it shouldn't be with the view to prove that you are right. Being right isn't the goal—peace is! Which means you must listen and endeavor to understand the other person's point of view.

In Proverbs 18:2 we are told, "A fool has no delight in understanding, but in expressing his own heart." In our pursuit of peace with people, we must strive to hear what they are saying and understand the **why** that lies behind their words or behavior.

And once you've listened and understood, here is an important phrase to remember: "I see what you are saying. I'm sorry." Not, "I'm sorry you're such an idiot," but just "I'm sorry" or "Will you forgive me?" It's actually quite shocking to see how many people have never learned to apologize. They offer the rose of an apology, but they make sure the people they are giving it to get pricked with a thorn.

As difficult as it might be for you to patiently listen to an offended party's point of view, it is well worth the effort. Listening with a view to understand and then sharing your feelings and view of things can pay off handsomely when the result is peace. Generally once people know they're being heard, they open their hearts to reconciliation and peace. But there will be times when words are not enough. So what do you do then?

## *A Powerful Tool of Communication*

Proverbs 19:7 brings out a truth that needs to be considered. It says, "All the brothers of the poor hate him; how much more do his friends go far from him! He may pursue them with words, yet they abandon him." Sometimes words are not enough. When words alone fail to open the door of peace with an offended party, perhaps it is time to deliberate the possibility of giving a gift.

Proverbs 18:16 proclaims, "A man's gift makes room for him, and brings him before great men." Other translations say, "A gift opens the way for the giver" (NIV 1984) and "Gifts can open many doors" (ERV).

Proverbs 21:14 says, "If anyone is angry with you, give them a gift in private. A gift given in secret will calm even the strongest anger" (ERV). The Message Bible puts it this way: "A quietly given gift soothes an irritable person; a heartfelt present cools a hot temper."

Generally, these verses are discussed in terms of bribery, but there is a positive side that we need to consider in our present context. Giving a gift can be a powerful tool of communication. Jacob pacified Esau's anger by giving him a series of gifts and in doing so saved his family (Genesis 32–33). Abigail brought gifts to David and prevented him from committing a grave sin in his anger. In doing so, she also preserved the lives of many innocent people (1 Samuel 25:14–35).

A friend of mine, who we'll call Sam, was driving in the car with another passenger while speaking to one of his key employees on the phone. We'll call him Ted. There were some difficulties in the office that my friend was unjustly blaming on Ted. And once the call was concluded, Sam turned to the passenger in the car and proceeded to say some very unkind things about Ted. They were things that should not have been said—**especially since he had failed to properly hang up the phone!**

The line was still open and Ted heard every unkind word that was said. When Sam reached the office, Ted walked into his office and presented him with a formal resignation as he said, "If that's what you truly think of me, I can find another place to work."

Sam was horrified when he learned that Ted had heard his angry words in the car. He asked for forgiveness and pleaded with Ted to stay, explaining that he had been speaking out of his anger and frustration of the moment and that he had been wrong. He pursued Ted with words, but his words fell short.

Sam then did something wise. He went out and bought Ted a gift. It wasn't expensive, but it opened a door that had been slammed shut. As he gave the gift, he again said he was sorry and that he had been wrong, and he asked Ted to change his mind about leaving. After a few moments of uncomfortable silence, Ted agreed to stay. Their relationship mended and they enjoyed several years of fruitful work together after that day.

The act of giving a gift, as we are looking at it now, is not about buying someone off or bribing them. As my friend Sam discovered, giving a gift can be a powerful form of communication, especially when someone has been wounded or offended. A gift can say, "I've thought about you. I have invested the time and effort to do this because I value you." As you pursue peace with people, be open to do more than just talk. If God should lead you to do so, enforce your earnestness to make things work with a gift. It need not be expensive, but it can be a powerful tool of communication just the same.

# ACTIONS

As we pursue peace with people, nothing speaks louder than our actions. If we really want to have peace with someone, giving them the cold shoulder, avoiding them, or acting like they are invisible will undo any positive influence that our verbal entreaties or gift giving might have wrought.

Our actions need to be inclusive, warm, and friendly. Invite the offended party to lunch if that is appropriate in your situation. Make them a part of your world. The old adage holds true: "Actions speak louder than words."

Even in marital relationships, 1 Peter 3:1 makes it clear that an unbelieving husband can be won to Christ by the behavior—not the preaching—of his wife. We have seen it happen many times in our own church. A woman comes to Christ and eventually—and sometimes rather rapidly—her husband accepts the Lord as well. I have heard many a man in essence say, "I couldn't get away from the transformation in her. She was more joyful, more loving, more patient with me. I waited for it to blow over, but soon realized that what she had was real and I wanted it."

If we really want to have peace with people, we will pray for them and talk with them. If needed and God so guides us, we can give a gift to them, and finally, we can endeavor to make them feel valued and accepted through our actions.

### *I Am for Peace, but They Are for War*

"But what if I earnestly do all I can to make peace with someone and they refuse?"

That is a possibility. Prayer will bring the Holy Spirit's influence upon a person's heart, but that does not remove his or her free will. Even God will not force a person to be saved against his or her will. If a person chooses to remain God's enemy and go into an eternity without Him, God will allow it.

In Psalm 120:7, King David laments, "I am for peace; but when I speak, they are for war." So it may be with some people in our lives. We cannot make people be at peace with us. We are only told to pursue peace.

Romans 12:18 says, "If it is possible, as much as depends on you, live peaceably with all men." Sometimes it will not be possible to have peace only because some may willfully refuse it. It is our responsibility to do our part and once we have done all we can do, all we can do has been done. We then must leave the outcome in God's hands.

However, if someone has made it clear that he or she will not reconcile and intends to remain opposed to you, that does not give you a license to treat this person badly. Romans 12:17–21 makes that clear: "Repay no one evil for evil. Have regard for good things in the sight of all men. If it is possible, as much as depends on you, live peaceably with all men. Beloved, do not avenge yourselves, but rather give place to wrath; for it is written, 'Vengeance is Mine, I will repay,' says the Lord. Therefore 'If your enemy is hungry, feed him; if he is thirsty, give him a drink; for in so doing you will heap coals of fire on his head.' Do not be overcome by evil, but overcome evil with good."

Dear friend, peace is possible. Because you have peace with God, you can know the peace of God. You can have peace instead of conflict with people, if you will begin to pursue peace. Our God is a God of peace; peace is His nature and His will for His people. It is His will for you.

# A PLAN FOR PURSUIT

And let the peace of God rule in your hearts, to which also you were called in one body; and be thankful.

Colossians 3:15

Thoughts, prayers, and questions to help you make a plan for pursuing peace:

- To keep you from pursuing peace with others, the enemy will often make you doubt the peace you have with God in Christ Jesus. Take some time to read Colossians 1:20 and declare in your heart: "I am loved, forgiven, and free because of the cross of Christ—at peace with God and empowered to pursue peace with those around me."

- Think of one person with whom you need to pursue peace. Read Mathew 5:44 and then take a moment to pray God's blessings over that person. Bring the love of Christ between you and them and ask God to fill their life with His grace and truth.

- One of the greatest obstacles to peace with others is our own pride and insistence that the situation is resolved with our vindication. If you've been avoiding peace because you want vindication first, confess that to God, express your trust in His timing to set all things right, and ask for His help to pursue peace in humility.

▸ What's one action you could take that would pave the way for peace between you and another person (maybe even between you and a group of people)? Maybe it's as simple as a kind or grateful post on Facebook. Maybe it entails a phone call or giving a gift. Whatever God puts on your heart, prayerfully follow through on that action today.

## THE PURSUIT OF THE KNOWLEDGE OF THE LORD

In John 17:3, Jesus described salvation perfectly when He said, "And this is eternal life, that they may know You, the only true God, and Jesus Christ whom You have sent." More than anything else, receiving eternal life, or being saved, is about knowing God.

That's why in calling the people of Israel back to a covenant relationship with God, the prophet Hosea cries out, "Let us know, **let us pursue the knowledge of the Lord.** His going forth is established as the morning; He will come to us like the rain, like the latter and former rain to the earth" (Hosea 6:3, emphasis mine).

The pursuit of the knowledge of the Lord reflects the heart attitude you and I should have today as believers.

God's plan is that we continually grow in knowledge and that our relationship with Him advances and deepens as time goes on. And since God is infinite, knowing Him is a never ending journey. Hosea also reveals a beautiful truth in that same verse quoted above: when we do pursue the knowledge of the Lord, He will come to us! We will be visited by His Spirit, which is what the figure of the latter and former rain refers to. The question then arises, **how do we pursue the knowledge of the Lord?**

# Methods of Pursuit

## NATURE

A good place for you to begin pursuing the knowledge of God is nature. Psalm 19:1 proclaims, "The heavens declare the glory of God; and the firmament shows His handiwork." The New Testament reveals the same truth in Romans 1:18–20 where it says, "But God shows his anger from heaven against all sinful, wicked people who suppress the truth by their wickedness. They know the truth about God because he has made it obvious to them. For ever since the world was created, people have seen the earth and sky. Through everything God made, they can clearly see his invisible qualities—his eternal power and divine nature. So they have no excuse for not knowing God" (NLT 2015).

Creation speaks to the human heart about the Creator. Personally, I would rather be outdoors than indoors—any day. I love to hike and fish. I love to be on the sea or to sit in my yard and watch the sunset or gaze at the stars at night. Without fail, nature seems to always whisper to my heart about the mysteries of God. And the Scriptures tell us to look at the birds, consider the lilies, and to observe the ants, for God has hidden lessons for us in all aspects of His creation.

Even Martin Luther declared that God had written the promise of resurrection on every leaf of springtime.

Of course, some people take their love of nature too far. Even some Christians use their love of the outdoors as an excuse not to attend church. "The sky is my cathedral, and the trees are my congregation," they say. Creation is wonderful and it should be enjoyed and learned from, but you cannot learn all you need to know about God from nature, and the Scripture commands us not to neglect gathering together (Hebrews 10:25). So, if nature is a starting point, where do we go from there?

## THE BIBLE

The Bible is a book of God's thoughts. It reveals His nature, His will, and His purpose for mankind. Through it, He brings us into a deep and abiding relationship with Himself. Without it, we are like a boat adrift on a sea of uncertainty only catching occasional glimpses of the shore. But when you read it and prayerfully reflect upon its truths—it is like an invitation to come ashore and explore the endless mysteries of who He is.

God has breathed His very life into His Word (2 Timothy 3:16). Jesus said that the words He spoke were spirit and life. When you study and meditate upon His Word, it does more than fill your head with knowledge. It leads to a progressive discovery and encounter with God Himself.

In the opening verses of his gospel, John declares, "In the beginning was the Word, and the Word was with God, and the Word was God. He was in the beginning with God. All things were made through Him, and without Him nothing was made that was made. In Him was life, and the life was the light of men. . . . And the Word became flesh and dwelt among us, and we beheld His glory, the glory as of the only begotten of the Father, full of grace and truth (John 1:1–4, 14).

God and His Word are one. Jesus is the Word made flesh. If we are truly going to pursue the knowledge of God, seeking to know Him more intimately, then we **must** spend regular, unhurried time in His Word.

## *A 35 Cent Investment That Changed My Life*

Probably the most significant thing about my personal relationship with God has been the place His Word has held in my life. After I was saved and bought my first Bible, I carried it with me almost everywhere I went and read it constantly. I obtained that first Bible in a yard sale for 35 cents and eventually wore it out. It changed my life.

I would stay up into the wee hours of the morning reading by candlelight because there was no electricity in the single room I was renting above the bar where I was living. No one told me that it might be wiser to begin reading in the New Testament, so I began in Genesis. I got a bit bogged down when I got to Leviticus but continued to slog my way through. An amazing thing began happening. God began to speak to my heart and reveal things to me about Himself that I still hold dear and rely upon to this very day.

Any fruit for the Kingdom, any good thing that has happened in or through my life, I attribute in large part to my love affair with God's book. If you don't have a Bible, get one. If you don't regularly read the one you have now, start.

It might even be a good practice to read it on your knees. It's a posture that says, "I am humbling myself to the truth of Your Word. I am taking it as my final authority on all matters of life. It is holy, and through it I am expecting to encounter the God who is one with it."

## PRAYER

What does prayer have to do with pursuing the knowledge of God?

The main reason for prayer is not to get things or to get out of things. It is not about us reading our latest Christmas list to our celestial Santa Claus. The main reason for prayer is to meet with God.

Looking again at our key Scripture in Hosea 6:3, it begins with the phrase "Let us **know**," followed by the command to "pursue the **knowledge** of the Lord." Both the words *know* and *knowledge* speak of an experiential knowledge, or knowledge gained through involvement. It's true that prayer needs to become a discipline and that sometimes our prayer times can seem as dead as a graveyard and as dry as a desert. But sometimes, as we pray, God is undeniably present in the sense that He becomes more real to us than anything else.

He is always present, we know, but sometimes He reveals Himself in startling, amazing, holy, and astonishing ways. In ways that almost defy description, in ways that make you weep as your heart can think of no other words besides "Holy, holy, holy is the Lord!"

### *"He's Real!"*

A friend of mine had come to Christ, but still struggled with some sinful habits from his old life. He began locking himself in his prayer closet for an hour and a half every morning before he went to work. Day after day he prayed. Though he found strength from his times of prayer, he still struggled. This went on for several weeks. Then one day he came over to my house, totally changed.

"He's real. He's real. He's real! He came to me in my prayer closet this morning! He's real!" He said it to me over and over. His countenance was glowing. I will never forget the look of absolute wonder and awe upon his face. Remember, Hosea 6:3 promises that when we pursue a personal intimate knowledge of Him, He will come to us.

Don't get me wrong. I know that He is always with us. In fact, as believers, He is dwelling within us. But I have also experienced visitations from Him in my life, as I prayed, where He revealed Himself in fuller, deeper ways.

He wants us to pursue Him. In fact, in Hosea 6:6 the Lord says, "For I desire mercy and not sacrifice, and the knowledge of God more than burnt offerings." God is not interested in empty ceremony or mindless religious rituals. He wants you to know Him. And as you pursue that knowledge, He will come to you!

## THOSE THAT WALK WITH GOD

You can also learn about God from wise people that walk with Him. Joshua learned of God through his association with Moses, Elisha from Elijah, and Timothy and Titus from Paul.

As a young believer, I learned key lessons about God from some older believers. The first was an eighty-year-old woman that everyone just called "Mom." She had started two orphanages in different countries and was raising six orphans in her home by herself. She also traveled and spoke at different churches, and she loved Jesus with all of her heart. I would occasionally come by and milk her goats for her and would end up having long conversations with her. She was a dynamo of strength. She taught me about the importance of consistent prayer, especially prayer in the spirit (see 1 Corinthians 14:4, 14–15, 18).

There was another older couple that talked in depth with me about the ministry of the Holy Spirit. They prayed for me and with me and during a critical time in my life, gave me some valuable counsel. I will be forever grateful for the spiritual impartation into my life from these seasoned saints of God. The things that God had strongly worked into their lives they passed on to me. That is something that God wants us all to do. Second Timothy 2:2 captures this principle well as Paul says, "And the things that you have heard from me among many witnesses, commit these to faithful men who will be able to teach others also."

Proverbs 13:20 says, "He who walks with wise men will be wise, but the companion of fools will be destroyed." We learn from those we associate with—both good and bad. And the truth is, we can only pass on to others what we have and who we are. And when it comes to the things of

God, you cannot reveal any more of God to someone else than you have experienced yourself.

## Raised by Buffalo Hunters

When I was at university in Oregon, I took a course on Native American religions and practices. It was taught by a middle-aged, guru wannabe, pot-smoking professor who really didn't have a clue about Native American life other than what he had read in books himself. For me, the class had little to offer and I found it hard to stay awake for the entire hour.

Sometime later I was visiting a remote town with some friends that was tucked away in the Oregon backcountry. As we were exploring a back street, we found a yard filled with some of the most amazing and unique furniture we had ever seen. An old man was sitting in the yard, so I struck up a conversation with him. As it turned out, he had fashioned every piece of furniture by hand. He invited us into his modest home and we ended up spending the entire afternoon with him. It was an eye-opening day.

He had been born around the turn of the century and orphaned as a little boy. Two old buffalo hunters adopted and raised him. The buffalo hunters had both been raised by Native Americans. They had passed all their firsthand knowledge of Native American life and ingenuity on to him. He spent the next few hours answering our questions and showing us some things we had never seen before.

With a piece of deer antler and a piece of obsidian, he made a perfect arrowhead in less than two minutes. He taught us how to do an ear-piercing whistle with a piece of bark or bit of stone between our fingers, and he went into detail about an amazing trick that would almost guarantee you a nice deer if you were out hunting.

We were mesmerized. This wasn't just something that he had read in a book somewhere; he had personal, experiential, intimate knowledge of the subject—unlike my university professor—and it made all the difference in the world.

One of the ways that God has chosen to reveal Himself is through those who know Him. Through preaching, teaching, and living out their faith, God uses men and women to open the eyes of others and impart the knowledge of the Lord to those with hungry hearts.

When I gave my heart to Christ in the little street mission in Medford, Oregon, I wasn't looking for a set of rules and regulations to adhere to or for some new doctrine to digest; I was looking for God. He revealed Himself to my heart that night in a way that forever changed my life. And He did it through the people who shared. One after another they stood behind a huge wooden lectern and "testified." I found a relationship with God that night through His Son, Jesus Christ, and the way He revealed Himself to me was through people who walked with Him.

So, as you pursue the knowledge of the Lord, He will come and reveal Himself to you. You can pursue this knowledge through nature, through the Bible, through prayer, and from the wise who walk with Him. It is the greatest of all pursuits.

We must pursue an intimate knowledge of God, not because He is hiding from us, but because He is hiding for us—waiting to reveal Himself to hungry hearts. As you begin to pursue Him, you will find, like Abraham of old, that God Himself is your exceedingly great reward (Genesis 15:1).

# A PLAN FOR PURSUIT

> Then you will understand the fear of the Lord, and find the knowledge of God. For the Lord gives wisdom; from His mouth come knowledge and understanding.
>
> Proverbs 2:5–6

Thoughts, prayers, and questions to help you make a plan for pursuing the knowledge of God:

- To know God is an invitation to drink deeply of the relationship you were created to enjoy forever. Are you ready to say yes to God's invitation? Take some time now to pray and tell God that you want your life to be characterized by the pursuit of knowing Him.

- The sixteenth century theologian and reformer John Calvin called nature the "theater of God's glory." It's an ongoing performance where you can see God's artistry on display. But you need to unplug and step out onto the stage. Make a commitment to get outside a few times a week and go on a prayer walk, just you and the Creator. You'll be amazed at what He reveals of Himself.

- Hebrews 4:12 says the Word of God is "living and powerful." That's because it is synonymous with the living and powerful God—to spend prayerful time in Scripture is to spend time with His Spirit. What does that time look like in your week? Is it consistent? Meaningful? Non-existent? Take a moment to look at your schedule and find a time you can dive into God's Word regularly.

▶ We tend to look for formulas when it comes to achieving some spiritual goal. But it's amazing how often we forget to voice that goal to God in prayer. God has invited you into a life-long journey of growing in the knowledge of Him, so let Him know you're ready. Share your heart's desire with God in prayer and ask Him to lead you forward in ever increasing knowledge.

Who do you know in your life that walks with God? How can you get around them more? Maybe you can't think of anyone. If so, ask God to bring someone into your life. Develop the habit of intentionally placing yourself in environments where you'll be sharpened by other believers. And embrace the chance to be that sharpening iron for others.

# THE PURSUIT OF HOSPITALITY

Let love be without hypocrisy. Abhor what is evil. Cling to what is good. Be kindly affectionate to one another with brotherly love, in honor giving preference to one another; not lagging in diligence, fervent in spirit, serving the Lord; rejoicing in hope, patient in tribulation, continuing steadfastly in prayer; distributing to the needs of the saints, given to hospitality.

Romans 12:9–13

In these verses we are given some very specific commands, but I just want to focus your attention on one: hospitality. We are in fact commanded in verse 13 to pursue hospitality. The word translated as *given* in that verse is the same Greek word translated *pursue* in 1 Peter 3:11 where we are told to *pursue* peace.

Hospitality literally means "to be fond of guests or to be friendly to strangers." As believers, you and I need to open our hearts and our homes to others. In fact, showing hospitality is one of the greatest means we have at our disposal for demonstrating the love of Christ.

## *Roast with Vegetables and a Game of Croquet*

After Janet and I were married and had a short honeymoon, we were in Wisconsin together where I had a speaking engagement. At the end of the service that Sunday, we found ourselves standing in the foyer alone. I had preached my heart out and prayed for several people, and when I was done, the pastor was gone. No mention had been made of an offering and we were flat broke. We were both hungry but didn't even have enough money to buy a hamburger.

As we stood there wondering what to do next, an elderly couple walked up to us and said, "Would you like to come to our house for lunch?" "Absolutely!" we responded, and they took us to their home for pot roast with vegetables. I will never forget their kindness. They made us feel at home and fed us like kings. I don't remember what I preached that day, but I do remember what I was served for lunch. I don't remember if anyone got saved, but I do remember an elderly couple that pursued hospitality. They impacted our lives in a significant way by demonstrating God's love to some young kids in ministry who were feeling a bit awkward and left out.

I remember another time, some years later, when I was conducting meetings in different cities in England. In one particular city, I spoke in a large church that had quite a history of influence for the gospel in that region. I had the whole family with me and we were on a fairly tight budget.

A couple from the church had volunteered to put our whole family up for the night.

Again, I don't remember what I preached, I don't even remember the senior pastor's name, but our whole family remembers the wonderful time we had at that couple's house, sharing a meal and a pot of tea and playing croquet in their backyard the next day in the English sunshine—laughter, more tea, and kindness that was tangible. Their hospitality affected us all. It's been nearly thirty years since that experience and my daughter still remembers it well.

Some people in the Church seem to pursue isolation rather than hospitality. Certainly, as with most things, there is a balance. There have been times when the guest beds in our home have never had enough time to get cold with so many people staying with us, but there have also been times of quiet where it has just been "Conley time," where we just hang out with family. It is important to be sensitive to when and when not to have guests in your home, but I think most people default on the side of being isolationists rather than pursuers of hospitality.

## The Why of Hospitality

The greatest reason for pursuing hospitality is because God's Word commands us to. The command in Romans 12:13 to practice and pursue hospitality is just that—a command, not a suggestion.

In addition to simple obedience, showing hospitality opens the door for new relationships and friendships to develop. You have yet to meet some of the greatest people that will enhance your life. When we host people in our homes or do something as simple as share a meal with someone, we have the privilege of spending unhurried time with them—unique individuals, created in God's image with unique stories and insights that they have picked up along their life's journey. Some of the most fascinating and helpful things can be learned as we show hospitality to people.

Hospitality is also a tangible way to demonstrate the love of God and the reality of your salvation to the person that needs more than words. As James 2:18 puts it, "I will show you my faith by my works." Your actions can preach a sermon to the hearts of people who are looking for God. Third John 5–8 says, "Dear friend, when you extend hospitality to Christian brothers and sisters, even when they are strangers, **you make the faith visible**" (MSG, emphasis mine).

We should keep in mind as well that whatever we do for the least and lowliest person, we do for Christ. Jesus Himself said, "'For I was hungry and you gave Me food; I was thirsty and you gave Me drink; **I was a stranger and you took Me in;** I was naked and you clothed Me; I was sick and you visited Me; I was in prison and you came to Me.' Then the righteous will answer Him, saying, 'Lord, when did we see You hungry and feed You, or thirsty and give You drink? **When did we see You a stranger and take You in,** or naked and clothe You? Or when did we see You sick, or in prison, and come to You?' And the King will answer and say to them, 'Assuredly, I say to you, **inasmuch as you did it to one of the least of these My brethren, you did it to Me**'" (Matthew 25:35–40, emphasis mine).

Finally, we should pursue hospitality because it may be a test. Your guest may very well be in disguise. The writer of Hebrews reminds us, "Do not forget to entertain strangers, for by so doing some people have entertained angels without knowing it" (Hebrews 13:2 NIV 1984).

## Persuasive, Sensitive, and Starting Small

Here are a few closing thoughts on the subject of pursuing hospitality:

Sometimes you're going to need to be persistent and persuasive in offering hospitality. Some people may refuse your hospitality—due to pride or not wanting to be a burden—when first offered, but they are secretly hoping that you will insist.

If you feel that God has led you to open your home to someone, be persuasive about it. Consider the story of when Paul and Silas first came to Macedonia. Lydia and her household had been won to the Lord and water baptized. In Acts 16:15 we read, "After she was baptized, along with everyone in her household, she said in a surge of hospitality, 'If you're confident that I'm in this with you and believe in the Master truly, come home with me and be my guests.' We hesitated, but she wouldn't take no for an answer" (MSG). Other translations say, "She urged us" (NLT) and "she persuaded us" (NKJV).

In 2 Corinthians 7:15 where Paul speaks to his readers about their treatment of Titus, he says, "He can't quit talking about it, going over again and again the story of your prompt obedience, and the dignity and sensitivity of your hospitality. He was quite overwhelmed by it all" (MSG).

Sensitivity is a big word when it comes to any dealings with people, especially in the arena of hospitality. People can feel quite awkward in someone else's home, like they are imposing on other's privacy or generosity. It is a gift when we can make people feel at ease.

I know some people who, upon reading this, will think: "But I only have a little apartment!" or "I don't have much to share." Hospitality starts in the heart and consists of sharing whatever God has blessed you with, be it great or small.

I have eaten roasted goat with a remote Indian tribe in the mountains of Mexico. They didn't have much at all. In fact, the goat we ate was an act of extravagant giving for them. I was made to feel like an honored guest among them, and to this day I treasure the memory of their kindness and hospitality toward me. I have also eaten delicate finger foods in what some would describe as a palace, surrounded by all the furnishings associated with excessive wealth where I was made to feel more like an intruder than anything else. True hospitality has more to do with what's in your heart than with any material things you possess.

If you don't practice hospitality, determine to start. Begin a pursuit of the art of being hospitable. Do what you can with what you have. Do your best to make people feel welcome and accepted. As you do, the Lord will take your kindness personally, and you may even end up entertaining angels without knowing it!

# A PLAN FOR PURSUIT

> Is it not to share your bread with the hungry, and that you bring to your house the poor who are cast out; when you see the naked, that you cover him, and not hide yourself from your own flesh?
>
> Isaiah 58:7

Thoughts, prayers, and questions to help you make a plan for pursuing hospitality:

- The passage above from Isaiah is about what true worship (or fasting) entails. In a word, it requires hospitality. To love God is to love others in His name. And that means caring for them in action.

- If we're honest, the only thing standing between us and choosing to be hospitable is our own heart. Sure, hospitality may look different for various people based on their circumstances and means, but the effort to care for others in the name of Jesus is something anyone can undertake. What might hospitality look like in your life?

- Consider the power of hospitality in today's divided culture. Many people have such a jaded view of Christians that the only way they'll hear and experience the true message of the gospel is if you **show** it to them through hospitality.

Ask God to bring you opportunities to show hospitality. Ask Him to give you His heart for those He brings your way. And pray that others would encounter Christ through you.

# 4

# THE PURSUIT OF WHAT IS GOOD

First Thessalonians 5:15 tells us, "See that no one renders evil for evil to anyone, but always pursue what is good both for yourselves and for all." This verse forbids us from paying back in kind those who have done evil to us. On the contrary, you and I are to always seek to do good to others—even to those who have done us serious harm.

Jesus made this same truth clear in His teaching where He said, "You have heard that it was said, 'You shall love your neighbor and hate your enemy.' But I say to you, love your enemies, bless those who curse you, do good to those who hate you, and pray for those who spitefully use you and persecute you, that you may be sons of your Father in heaven; for He makes His sun rise on the evil and on the good, and sends rain on the just and on the unjust" (Matthew 5:43–45). Doing good, especially to those who have done us evil, is one of the things that sets us apart and makes us recognizable as God's children.

I heard it said once that there are three classes of people. First, there is the person who renders evil for good. Second, there is the person who renders good for good. And third, there is the person of God who renders good for evil. Let us seek to be in this third class of people, whose behavior mirrors that of our Father in heaven.

## For Yourselves and for All

What does Paul mean in 1 Thessalonians 5:15 when he says, "Pursue what is good both for **yourselves** and for **all**"?

Pursuing what is good for yourselves and for all can be looked at two ways. First, *yourselves* can refer to the community of believers, the Church, while *all* refers to the unsaved world outside of the Church. We need to be concerned about and look to the welfare of the Church but also to the welfare of the community in which the local church resides.

Another way to understand this verse is that *yourselves* refers to each member of the Church as an individual, and *all* refers to everyone else. I am going to deal with the verse in this light because it makes the responsibility personal. In other words, as I pursue what is good for me, I must always weigh how my actions, my words, and my methods of pursuing what is good for me affect others. How is my pursuit affecting my spouse, my family, my friends, the Church, my neighbors, and the community? I have the liberty to look out for myself **but not at the expense of others.**

Many times, as people pursue personal advantages they knowingly hurt others along the way. Yet they defend their position with statements like, "Well, I need this. It's good for me. I deserve this. I have to think about myself." Okay, in the light we are looking at it, 1 Thessalonians 5:15 allows for that and even encourages you in the pursuit of what is good for you, but it adds the proviso **"and for all,"** which cannot be overlooked. If what is good for you is detrimental to others, you need to rethink your present course.

How blessed the world would be, how blessed the Church would be, how blessed our homes would be if we began to practice this! Imagine if in the pursuit of our personal good, we always thought, "How will my actions affect those around me? While doing what is necessary to procure good for my life, how can I do things that will bring a benefit to all?"

## Speaking Engagements, Golf, and Spearfishing

A good friend of mine is the founding pastor of a huge church in the northwestern part of our country. Early on, his church experienced explosive growth and became one of the "hot topics" in many Christian circles. Invitations began to pour in for my friend to come and speak at conventions and churches, both across the U.S. and around the world. He authored several books that sold quite well, and the honorariums he was given for speaking at various events added up to a significant yearly sum. It was good for him. He was well known and well paid. But it turned out not to be good for all.

It wasn't too long before he realized that being gone so much on assorted speaking engagements wasn't healthy for his own flock nor was it good for his family. Even though the popularity and big offerings could have been put in the plus column for him personally, his frequent absences due to speaking engagements were definitely in the minus column for his congregation, his wife, and his small children.

He weighed things out in the light of what was **good for all** and greatly curtailed his outside speaking schedule. The result was a happy marriage, a solid home, and a healthy congregation that continued to grow.

I lead a very busy life. My wife and I pioneered and still play a significant role in a church of multiple thousands. Along with my responsibilities to that flock, I also travel and speak, write books, and broadcast a global television ministry that is translated into multiple languages. I could spend twenty-four hours a day doing ministry work and it would still never all be done.

In order to let off steam and relax, I pursue a couple of hobbies. First, there is golf. I love it. Walking a course for several hours with friends is good for my soul. But there is a second hobby I pursue that I love even more. I am a free diver. I love to swim in the ocean, speargun in hand. Several friends and I go out fairly often on spearfishing adventures or to catch lobsters. I find the challenge of holding my breath while trying to catch dinner for the night to be extremely beneficial, both physically and emotionally. I call it "saltwater therapy."

However, as much as I like to golf or free dive, I always try to weigh things out in light of what the season looks like that I'm in at that moment. Do I need to be spending more time with my wife or with family? Is getting away on an overnight dive trip good for **all** right now? Honestly, I believe that the hobbies I pursue are not just a luxury; they are a necessity for my physical, emotional, and spiritual health. They help me be more of a balanced person and actually add to the impact I have in ministry. But I can't just go any time I want to. Sometimes pursuing the things I love are not good for all. Sometimes I just need to hang out with Janet, or it may be a season when a lot of extra work or study is required for ministry at the church. That same biblical balance is something my wife pursues as well. It's so important for her to take time to do things with her friends or by herself that fill up her emotional and spiritual tank. The key behind each choice is the principle of weighing your pursuits by what is good for **yourself** and for **all.**

The best scenario is when pursuing what is good for you becomes a win for everybody. That may not always be possible and the benefits that are derived may not always be equal for all, but it should be your goal to live your life with a "good for all" mentality. God will bless you for it.

Although it is important to pursue the things that make for a healthy you, in that pursuit you must always consider others. God wants to bless you in every arena of life, and He will lead you in making the necessary steps to lead a blessed life. But as you pursue what is personally good for you and you stay committed to doing it God's way, you will find that instead of pushing others down or out of the way, you'll actually lift them up.

# A PLAN FOR PURSUIT

Let nothing be done through selfish ambition or conceit, but in lowliness of mind let each esteem others better than himself.

Philippians 2:3

Thoughts, prayers, and questions to help you make a plan for pursuing what is good:

- Do you trust that God's heart for you is truly for your good? That He wants you to be happy? In his book *The Great Divorce,* C. S. Lewis writes that God created you for "infinite happiness." The problem is we often pursue that happiness (or good) outside of God's designed parameters—and chase after our good at others' expense. But what if "infinite happiness" comes from God's hand when we trust His love for us and pursue the good of others?

- Examine the pace and schedule of your life. How is it affecting your emotional, physical, and spiritual health? How is it affecting your loved ones? Take some time to ask God to shed His light on your situation and reveal whether or not it's leading to your own good and the good of those around you.

- Can you think of someone in your life that you can put first today? What could you do to pursue their good, even above your own? Ask God to help you take that step today.
- Consider how your witness for Christ might be put on display if you began to live more intentionally with a "good for all" mentality. Would that make the gospel attractive to today's culture? How could you pursue that path in your community?

# 5

# THE PURSUIT OF LOVE

> Pursue love, and desire spiritual gifts, but especially that you may prophesy.
>
> 1 Corinthians 14:1

A large, very thick book could be written on the pursuit of love alone. It could be applied to salvation, marriage, family, trusting God, casting out fear, dealing with enemies, getting along with people in the Church, and on and on. I am only going to deal with the subject of love, however, as we find it here in the context of the operation of the gifts of the Spirit.

The exhortation to pursue love in 1 Corinthians 14:1 is found right in the middle of an extensive teaching on the gifts of the Spirit. In fact, 1 Corinthians 12–14 deals with the gifts of the Spirit. Chapter 12 gives us the definitions of the gifts, chapter 13 tells us the spirit that should characterize their use, and chapter 14 gives us guidelines for their operation in the local church.

For the purpose of study, the gifts can be divided into three different categories. There are three gifts that say something (the utterance gifts), three gifts that reveal something (the revelation gifts), and three gifts that do something (the power gifts).

The three gifts that say something are, first, **prophecy**, whereby someone speaks to men by the inspiration of the Spirit to bring edification, exhortation, and comfort (1 Corinthians 12:10; 14:3).

The second, **different kinds of tongues,** means a supernatural utterance in an unknown tongue. According to 1 Corinthians 13:1, it may be the tongues of men or angels, but it is unknown to the speaker. Finally, the **interpretation of tongues** is the supernatural speaking out of the meaning of an utterance in tongues (1 Corinthians 12:10).

The three gifts that reveal something are **the word of knowledge,** which is the revelation by the Spirit concerning past or present facts. It is where the Holy Spirit reveals something to a believer apart from human aid. It is not learned knowledge. It is—like all nine of these gifts—supernatural. **The word of wisdom** is a supernatural revelation by the Spirit to a believer concerning the plans and purposes of God. This gift deals with future events. Finally, there is **the discerning of spirits,** where a believer is given insight—or temporary sight—into the spirit realm. By this gift, one can, as the Spirit wills, discern angels or demons and the work they are doing.

The three gifts that do something, commonly referred to as the power gifts, are **faith**, or "special faith" as the New Living Translation puts it (1 Corinthians 12:9 NLT 1996).

General faith, or "saving faith," comes by hearing and can be developed and increased by exercising it in the arena of life (Romans 10:17; Ephesians 2:8–9; 2 Thessalonians 1:3). But the gift of special faith is given as the Spirit wills (1 Corinthians 12:11). It is a special, temporary endowment by the Spirit of extraordinary faith that will keep and protect you in extraordinary circumstances. **The gifts of healings** invoke the supernatural healing of disease without any medical means (1 Corinthians 12:9). And finally, **the working of miracles** is a supernatural intervention into the ordinary course of nature through the power of the Holy Spirit whereby the laws of nature are suspended or altered.

There are some marvelous resources whereby you can learn about the gifts of the Spirit and their operation in detail. *Questions and Answers on Spiritual Gifts* by Howard Carter was one that really helped me when I first came to Christ. It is a worthwhile and important study as it is one subject that we are specifically told not to be ignorant about (1 Corinthians 12:1).

There is something of even greater power that fuels the use and impact of these gifts, something that you and I must pursue with abandon . . . love.

## Love Should Characterize Their Use

After telling us how the Spirit distributes the gifts among the body as He determines, and after we are told to eagerly desire the gifts, 1 Corinthians 12 ends with these words: "And yet I show you a more excellent way" (v. 31). And that way is love. It is the attitude that should undergird and permeate the heart of the believer as he or she is used to operate in the gifts.

> Though I speak with the tongues of men and of angels, but have not love, I have become sounding brass or a clanging cymbal. And though I have the gift of prophecy, and understand all mysteries and all knowledge, and though I have all faith, so that I could remove mountains, but have not love, I am nothing. And though I bestow all my goods to feed the poor, and though I give my body to be burned, but have not love, it profits me nothing. (1 Corinthians 13:1–3)

Paul is still talking about the gifts in this passage. Tongues and the interpretation of tongues, the gift of prophecy, the word of knowledge, and the word of wisdom are referred to as well as the gift of faith. The thing he is emphasizing is the spirit or attitude that should characterize their use. The gift can be genuine, but if I'm not walking in love, my prophesying becomes little more than noise. The water that flows through the hose picks up some of the taste of the hose. Yes, these gifts are Holy Spirit inspired and imparted, but they still flow through fallible, human vessels.

I remember a woman who would occasionally prophesy in church. What she said was always good, but it always seemed to have the effect of something jagged being slowly dragged across a chalkboard. It was terrible and we always dreaded the moment she would begin to speak. As it turned out—surprise, surprise—she had some deep-seated issues of unforgiveness and anger with her family. I truly believe the gift she was operating in was genuine; it's just that the hose it had to flow through had some nasty things that needed to be cleaned out of it.

The Spirit may want to use you to bring blessing to the body through the gifts, but it is up to you to walk in love. It is up to you to be a clean vessel through which He can flow. According to 1 Corinthians 13:2, even if I am operating in all three categories of gifts—utterance, revelation, and power—if I don't have love, **I am nothing.** It didn't say that the gifts weren't genuine; the problem is me and my lack of love. From heaven's point of view, we are defined by our character, not our accomplishments. Even if others gain some profit, if our hearts are wrong, we will not profit or be rewarded for operating in the gifts or for our personal sacrifice (1 Corinthians 13:3).

## What God's Love in Us Looks Like

"Well, everyone's got his or her own definition of love," someone says. That may be true, but that person's definition may not be true. Right here, in the following verses, we are given a definition of what God's love in us is supposed to look like. This is what you and I are supposed to be pursuing:

> Love endures long and is patient and kind; love never is envious nor boils over with jealousy, is not boastful or vainglorious, does not display itself haughtily. It is not conceited (arrogant and inflated with pride); it is not rude (unmannerly) and does not act unbecomingly. Love (God's love in us) does not insist on its own rights or its own way, for it is not self-seeking; it is not touchy or fretful or resentful;

> it takes no account of the evil done to it [it pays no attention to a suffered wrong]. It does not rejoice at injustice and unrighteousness, but rejoices when right and truth prevail.
>
> Love bears up under anything and everything that comes, is ever ready to believe the best of every person, its hopes are fadeless under all circumstances, and it endures everything [without weakening]. Love never fails [never fades out or becomes obsolete or comes to an end]. (1 Corinthians 13:4–8 AMPC)

Did you notice that it said, "Love (God's love in us) does not insist on its own rights"? According to Romans 5:5, the love of God has already been poured into the heart of the believer. The ability to do everything you just read in 1 Corinthians 13:4–8 is already in you! When we consider the command to "pursue love," it's not about pursuing something that is vacant from our lives. If we belong to Christ, the love of God has already been deposited into our hearts. It is a part of our new nature as Christians.

We are to pursue the expression of that love, of our new nature (2 Corinthians 5:17), and purposely let it work its way into our actions and words. "How is it done?" you might ask. In the simplest of terms, the answer is **you make a choice to do so.** The love of God in you is either turned loose or held on a leash by the power of choice.

There is, however, a key to developing a life that exemplifies God's love. It is a vital part of letting your new nature dominate your words and actions. That key is consistently feeding upon and renewing your mind with the Word of God.

## A Steady Diet of God's Word

In Paul's first letter to the Corinthians, he told them that they were acting just like unsaved men, being dominated by their fleshly desires. And the reason they were not walking in love or demonstrating their new inward nature as believers was because they had not had a steady diet of the Word.

> Brothers and sisters, when I was there, I could not talk to you the way I talk to people who are led by the Spirit. I had to talk to you like ordinary people of the world. You were like babies in Christ. And the teaching I gave you was like milk, not solid food. I did this because you were not ready for solid food. And even now you are not ready. You are still not following the Spirit. You are jealous of each other, and you are always arguing with each other. This shows that you are still following your own selfish desires. You are acting like ordinary people of the world. (1 Corinthians 3:1–3 ERV)

What was true of the Corinthians is true of many in the Church today. They have been thoroughly saved, their spirit has had a new birth experience, but their mind remains unrenewed. They have never had a steady diet of God's Word to feed and strengthen their spirit or to change their thinking. Consequently, their flesh, which still has the nature of sin in it, rules their conduct.

If we are to grow in Christ—and demonstrate the love nature that has already been poured into our hearts—we must make feeding on God's Word a daily business. A well-fed spirit and a renewed mind will always be victorious in putting the body and its fleshly desires under subjection (Romans 12:1–2; 1 Corinthians 9:27). Pursuing love means making choices—choices that become much easier as you fill your mind and feed your spirit with the Word of God.

There is a story told of a man that had been plagued with severe physical symptoms for some months. He went to the doctor and had a thorough examination. After several days he got a call to come to the doctor's office to find out the results of his exam. He and his wife went.

The doctor called his wife into a separate room and said, "The tests we did on your husband revealed that he has a rare form of anemia, which could prove fatal if he does not get lots of rest and a healthy diet. If you will make sure that he gets a hot breakfast every morning, a good lunch, and a wholesome dinner every night, it could make all the difference in the world. Also, his immune system has been very weakened, so it's important that you keep the house spotless. If you do these things your husband has a good chance that he will make it. Would you like to break the news to him, or should I?" asked the doctor.

The wife said, "I'll tell him." She went out in the waiting room and when her husband saw her face, he said, "It's bad isn't it?" Tears welled up in her eyes and she blurted out, "Yes, the doctor says you're going to die!"

Obviously, that wife wasn't willing to make the choice that would benefit her husband. May we be different, allowing the love of God to dominate our words and actions. What a difference it will make—especially as God uses us in the gifts of the Spirit. They will have a far greater impact when they flow out of a life of love.

## A Good Practice

A great starting place for allowing God's love to dominate your heart and mind is right where we have been reading in 1 Corinthians 13. If you have struggled at all in the area of love, I would like to challenge you to do something. Quote these verses every morning when you get up and every night before you go to bed—and make it personal. Insert yourself into the verses because, as we have already seen, this is part of your new nature.

For your convenience, I have listed 1 Corinthians 13:4–8 below based on the Amplified Bible Classic Edition, but I have changed the verses slightly in order to make them personalized. Say them out loud. If you belong to Christ, what you will be saying is in you. Let it out!

> I endure long and am patient and kind. I never am envious or boil over with jealousy. I am not boastful or vainglorious, and I do not display myself haughtily. I am not conceited (arrogant and inflated with pride). I am not rude (unmannerly) and do not act unbecomingly. I do not insist on my own rights or my own way. I am not self-seeking. I am not touchy or fretful or resentful. I take no account of the evil done to me. I pay no attention to a suffered wrong. I do not rejoice at injustice and unrighteousness, but rejoice when right and truth prevail. I bear up under anything and everything that comes. I am ever ready to believe the best of every person, my hopes are fadeless under all circumstances, and I endure everything without weakening. I never fail.

At the beginning of this chapter we saw that we are to "pursue love, and desire spiritual gifts" (1 Corinthians 14:1). I believe that when it comes to the operation of the gifts of the Spirit in our lives, God meets us at the level of our desire. Let me encourage you by saying there is more. God wants to do more, and He wants His people to experience more of the gifts of His Spirit. Learn about them. Pray that they will function in your church and through your life, and as you seek God concerning His gifts, don't forget to pursue peace. They work hand in hand.

## A PLAN FOR PURSUIT

And we have known and believed the love that God has for us. God is love, and he who abides in love abides in God, and God in him.

1 John 4:16

Thoughts, prayers, and questions to help you make a plan for pursuing love:

- What spiritual gifts have you been entrusted with? Can you think of a time when you've exercised them without love? A time when you shared them in love? How did the experiences and results differ?

- There may be different expressions of love in different relationships, but all love that is truly love must reflect God's love. There simply is no other definition of love. Can you think of some ways love often gets perverted by sin in our culture? How does that affect the health of the relationships in which it's practiced?

- Take a moment to dwell on this simple truth: God really does love you. Accept it. Thank God for it. And rejoice in it today. Because it's His love that empowers you to love like Him. As 1 John 4:19 says, "We love Him because He first loved us."

- Who can you show love to today? What will it look like? Once you've considered someone, pray over them, and take steps today to reach out and love them like Jesus does.

# 6

# THE PURSUIT OF RIGHTEOUSNESS AND GODLINESS

> Now godliness with contentment is great gain. For we brought nothing into this world, and it is certain we can carry nothing out. And having food and clothing, with these we shall be content. But those who desire to be rich fall into temptation and a snare, and into many foolish and harmful lusts which drown men in destruction and perdition. For the love of money is a root of all kinds of evil, for which some have strayed from the faith in their greediness, and pierced themselves through with many sorrows. But you, O man of God, flee these things and **pursue righteousness, godliness, faith, love, patience, gentleness.**
>
> 1 Timothy 6:6–11 (emphasis mine)

In verse 11, Timothy is given six specific things to pursue. But before he is told to pursue them, he is told to flee. You can't pursue the right things until you flee from the wrong things. Here, in context, the wrong things are greed and having money and wealth as the all-consuming priority of life.

According to verse 9, those who desire to be rich—who make it their main priority in life—not only fall into temptation and a snare, but also end up drowned in destruction (ruin in this life) and perdition (ruin in the life to come). The truth is, if you're running after gold, you can't run after God. If you're pursuing riches, you can't pursue righteousness. If your heart's focus is on things, it can't be focused on the Creator of all things.

The Lord said to Ezekiel, "As for you, son of man, your people who talk of you by the walls and in the doors of the houses say one to another, every one to his brother, Come and hear what the word is that comes forth from the Lord. And they come to you as people come, and they sit before you as My people, and they hear the words you say, but they will not do them; for with their mouths they show much love, **but their hearts go after and are set on their [idolatrous greed for] gain.** Behold, you are to them as a very lovely [love] song of one who has a pleasant voice and can play well on an instrument, for they hear your words but do not do them" (Ezekiel 33:30–32 AMPC, emphasis mine).

The people enjoyed Ezekiel's preaching, but they didn't act upon it. They were going through the motions of having a relationship with God, but there was no substance to it. Why? Because their hearts were set on the pursuit of wealth. The Message Bible says, "They flatter you with compliments, but all they care about is making money and getting ahead" (vv. 30–32). The Living Bible says, "They talk very sweetly about loving the Lord, but with their hearts they are loving their money" (v. 31).

It comes down to these simple questions: What are you following after? What is your heart's greatest pursuit? And yes, we need to work and we need to work hard, and we need to be wise and pursue knowledge and experience so that we can be our best at whatever we do in order to command the highest pay possible for our skills and services. Nevertheless, making money should not be the great goal of our lives.

Even if you talk to someone that has the gift of giving described in Romans 12:8, you will find that money is not their focus. They may have special insight into financial matters and may even be entrusted with large sums of money, but to them the goal is spreading the gospel and being used by God to enrich the lives of others. They look at making money and being used by God to support kingdom work with their resources as a holy endeavor. To them, it's not just about making another dollar or buying themselves a bigger house.

We brought nothing into this world and we will carry nothing out. Our greatest treasures must be found in God. If we seek Him and His kingdom first, all the temporal things that people tend to worry about will be added to us (Matthew 6:31–33).

We've looked at something Paul urges believers to flee, but what kingdom things are we told to pursue in 1 Timothy 6? In order, they are righteousness, godliness, faith, love, patience, and gentleness. First on the list is **righteousness,** and that's what we'll discuss in the next section.

## Root and Fruit: Righteousness

Trees have both roots and fruit. The fruit that is produced upward is the result of the roots that go downward. Both the roots and the fruit are part of the same tree. So it is with righteousness.

The root of righteousness is what we receive as a gift at salvation. When we were saved, we were made righteous before God. It is not the result of our good works nor is it the result of spiritual maturity or growth. We do not increase or grow in our righteousness—as we have been given the very righteousness of Christ Himself. This righteousness enables us to come boldly into our heavenly Father's presence without any sense of shame or guilt. Oh, the wonder of Christ's sacrifice and gift to men (Romans 3:21–24; 5:15–19; 2 Corinthians 5:21)!

The Scriptures also speak of the "fruit" aspect of righteousness. That is where it is lived out. In 1 Timothy 6, Paul is speaking about the fruit of righteousness, or the quality of **character that has a right relationship with God as its foundation.** One translation puts it as pursuing "uprightness," while another says, "right living."

To paraphrase it we could say, "In all your dealings with people pursue uprightness, fairness, and honesty." It is set in stark contrast with those who will bend the rules and violate their conscience as they greedily pursue gain.

Pursuing uprightness and honesty in business not only honors God, it is also a way to let your light shine for Christ. In addition to these crucial issues, when people experience integrity, they will tell others. Whenever a person has received a "fair shake" from someone, they almost always talk about their experience with a friend. It's some of the best advertising a business . . . or the gospel . . . can get.

Personally, I can say that wherever I have found someone to be fair and forthright in his or her trade, I have happily sent this person loads of other customers.

## Buying Cars and Keeping Score

Janet and I are friends with a Christian man that runs a large car dealership. We have obtained several cars over the years through his business. In his showroom, hanging on the wall, is a large document signed by all the employees. It states that they all agree to treat their customers with fairness and integrity, to provide excellent service, and to maintain an attitude of helpfulness and kindness to everyone that comes their way. I was impressed when I first read it, but I have been more impressed to see it lived out over the many years that we have been buying cars from them. As believers, we must pursue and prize righteousness in all things.

In chapter four of this book, dealing with pursuing what is good, I mentioned that I like to play golf. It is a great way to get to know people, as you generally spend four to five hours either walking or riding together around the course. There are a few people that occasionally call me for a game, however, that I don't like to play with. The reason is because **they cheat!**

One man moves his ball constantly throughout the round. If it ends up in a divot, he moves it. If it ends up in the deep rough, he moves it a few inches and improves his lie. If he has an awkward stance in a bunker, he moves the ball to get a better stance. Then to top it off, after adding up the scores, he announces, "Bayless, I shot a seventy-nine! I beat you by two strokes." I smile, but all the while I'm thinking inside, "Liar! If you would have played your ball where it laid, you would have added six strokes to your score easily!" You can learn a lot about a man on a golf course.

Pursuing righteousness is not just about the big things or the public things in life. It's about the little things as well, including the private things that no one else sees. Because the truth is, you can't really compartmentalize your character. If you lack integrity in one area of your life, you simply lack integrity—and as much as you might try and keep certain aspects of your life separate from each other, what happens in one area always bleeds into the next.

Proverbs 11:18 declares, "The wicked man does deceptive work, but he who sows righteousness will have a sure reward." Play by the rules in sport and in business. Don't cut corners, put in an honest day's work, give people what they pay for and more. Pursue righteousness even when it's not convenient or popular.

When you pursue and practice righteousness, God will always see to it that it will eventually come back to you. Hosea 10:12 brings that out where it states, "Sow for yourselves righteousness, reap the fruit of unfailing love, and break up your unplowed ground; for it is time to seek the Lord, until he comes and showers righteousness on you" (NIV 1984). If you sow righteousness—uprightness, fairness, and honesty—God will see to it that the same is showered upon you at the proper time (see also Galatians 6:7).

Years ago, I met a man that had an unusually clean and state-of-the-art auto shop. His business was located in a small town that I frequented, and frankly it stood head and shoulders above the surrounding businesses in both appearance and functionality. I came to find out that the shop, in part, had been paid for by an old woman. She had been a customer of the owner. He had always treated her honestly and never gouged her in price, though other businesses in the area had done so. She and the owner became friends and when she died, she left her entire inheritance to him, which was a tidy sum, stating that he had been the only person she had ever dealt with who treated her with absolute integrity. He had sown the seeds of blessing and righteousness, and God saw that the same was showered upon him in the proper time.

### *The Miracle in Columbus, Ohio*

The following story was written by Isabel Wilkerson and published in *The New York Times* on November 24, 1987:

> COLUMBUS, Ohio, Nov. 22—At 9:30 A.M. on Oct. 28, a miracle happened here. It was the kind of thing people pray for or dream of but figure will never in a million years happen to them.
>
> That morning, traffic was normal on Interstate 71 when the back door of an armored truck suddenly

flew open and bags of money spilled out. Cars behind the truck hit the bags, splitting them open, and hundreds of thousands of dollars rained over the highway for more than a mile.

When motorists realized that it was not maple leaves but $100 bills blowing about, they braked in the middle of the highway to help clean up. People on nearby ramps jumped over guard rails to get to the money. The word went out on CB radios. People came from across town. They stuffed $20's, $50's and $100 bills in coat pockets, pants pockets and purses and carted whole bundles to their cars, smiling and praising their good fortune.

Now, the authorities trying to track down the money are having considerably less success persuading those people to come forward.

A million dollars blew over Interstate 71 that day. The officials have pleaded with residents to return the money willingly, and the armored truck company has even offered a 10 percent reward. So far, only about $100,000 has come in.

The officials say they will prosecute any thieving motorist they can find. But if public reaction is any indication, the armored car company may never see the remaining $900,000. Some people have already called the newspaper to vow not to give the money back. One man said he was set for life and leaving town.

The Metropolitan Armored Car Company has declined to say if the bills were marked, but officials hope to identify suspects from pictures taken by a passerby. The photos show people stooping over money that sits thick as a yard-full of leaves. One shows a woman kneeling on the freeway. "She's either praying or she's scooping up a lot of money," a police detective told a reporter after the money spill.

The incident has taught many here that, when temptation lights on your windshield, anyone can weaken, even people in this pillar of Midwestern integrity.[1]

Obviously, this story only underscores the world's need to see examples of righteousness. May God's Church provide those examples as men and women lead Christ-like lives of integrity and honesty, passionately pursuing righteousness in the big and small, the seen and unseen arenas of life.

## When Only the Lord Sees: Godliness

"But you, O man of God, flee these things and **pursue** righteousness, **godliness,** faith, love, patience, gentleness" (1 Timothy 6:11, emphasis mine). Godliness stems from the inward posture of being devout or reverent toward God. It has to do with maintaining a continual awareness of God and striving to live a life that is pleasing to Him.

Where righteousness deals more with our direct interaction with men, godliness leans more toward what we do before

---

[1] Isabel Wilkerson, "Code of Highway: Finders Keepers," *The New York Times*, November 24, 1987, https://www.nytimes.com/1987/11/24/us/columbus-journal-code-of-highway-finders-keepers.html.

God when no one else sees us. Because of that constant awareness of His presence and a desire to be more like Him, we continually pursue attitudes and decisions that will glorify Him.

Years ago, I read *In His Steps, What Would Jesus Do?* by Charles M. Sheldon. It is one of the best-selling books of all time, having sold over thirty million copies. The story is both fascinating and quite challenging. It is the story of a pastor who challenges his congregation to not do anything for a whole year without first asking, "What would Jesus do?" The effect this has on the different characters in the story forces the reader to deeply consider their own habits and life, especially if they claim to be a follower of Jesus. That book and the idea it puts forth illustrate what true godliness is all about.

The exhortation to **pursue** godliness is very appropriate because it is not found along the path of least resistance or by doing what comes naturally to our flesh. It truly must be pursued. In fact, it is rarely an easy road to follow. Pursuing a life of godliness guarantees certain hardships. Consider 2 Timothy 3:12: "Yes, and all who desire to live godly in Christ Jesus will suffer persecution." There is no getting around it. Godliness brings difficulty.

I have a friend named Jeff who lives in St. Louis, and I occasionally do some largemouth bass fishing with him. I love fishing with Jeff because he's not afraid to make the long, hard hikes to the best ponds. Sometimes after we have hoofed it cross-country for a while, we arrive sweaty, shins bleeding—and generally carrying a tick or two as unwanted passengers—at some of the most productive, secluded ponds that I have ever fished. The journey is uncomfortable, but the destination makes it worthwhile.

The pursuit of godliness can be looked at in the same way. The benefits far outweigh the difficulties.

Here are just a few of the benefits promised to those who pursue godliness:

> ***Contentment***—"Now godliness with contentment is great gain" (1 Timothy 6:6).
>
> ***Being set apart by and for God***—"But know that the Lord has set apart for Himself him who is godly" (Psalm 4:3).
>
> ***Deliverance from temptation***—"The Lord knows how to deliver the godly out of temptations" (2 Peter 2:9).
>
> ***Profits both now and in the life to come***—"But reject profane and old wives' fables, and exercise yourself toward godliness. For bodily exercise profits a little, but godliness is profitable for all things, having promise of the life that now is and of that which is to come" (1 Timothy 4:7–8).

That last promise really demands our consideration. First, it makes it obvious that godliness requires work. In fact, the word *exercise* is the Greek word used to describe the rigorous training carried out by Olympic athletes. Second, it alludes to benefits derived both on earth and in heaven for those who grow in godliness.

## Heaven Is the Great Equalizer

I like to think of heaven as the great equalizer. Yes, God promises rewards to the godly in this life, but the lion's share of reward will certainly be found in the life to come. No one will stand in eternity and say, "Serving God wasn't worth it. Obedience to the Word wasn't worth it. Denying my flesh and living a godly life wasn't worth it. I feel cheated." No one in heaven will ever consider uttering such things because the rewards will be so great.

Years ago, as a young Christian, I worked as a waiter in a restaurant. At the end of each shift we were supposed to fill out a form stating how much we had earned in tips for the day. We were then taxed accordingly, which was reflected in our weekly paycheck. Sometimes I would end up averaging a little over a dollar per hour on my paycheck after they had taken out the taxes for my tips.

All the other waiters became very angry with me because the amounts they were claiming to have made in tips were always far less—usually about ten times less—than what I was reporting. It wasn't that I got bigger tips; they just lied about what they received so they wouldn't have to pay the taxes. They had a representative come to me on their behalf to ask me to stop reporting the full amount because it exposed their dishonesty. I refused. It caused a fair bit of harassment for me on the job and some public ridicule at the employee Christmas party, but knowing that I was doing the godly thing made it worthwhile, and God certainly rewarded me for it in a number of ways.

I realize that the minimal persecution I received at that job can in no way be compared to the savage persecution that some of our brothers and sisters experience for their faith throughout the world. Which brings me back to the point at hand. Godliness not only holds a promise for this life, but also for the life to come. Anything suffered in the pursuit of godliness will be written down in heaven's books and thoroughly rewarded in eternity.

In the following two chapters we'll complete Paul's list to Timothy of that which is worthy for every believer to pursue, picking up next with the pursuit of faith and love.

Before we get to our "A Plan for Pursuit" at the end of this chapter, let me reemphasize two things: 1) pursuing righteousness deals more with our outward actions toward people while 2) pursuing godliness deals more with our inward posture toward God. The Christian life is both inward and outward. We live for God with inward purity and purpose, but that life is always expressed outwardly before men. God's watching and so are people. Pursuing righteousness and godliness will pay off, both in this life and in the life to come.

# A PLAN FOR PURSUIT

"But seek first the kingdom of God and His righteousness, and all these things shall be added to you."

Matthew 6:33

Thoughts, prayers, and questions to help you make a plan for pursuing righteousness and godliness:

- You may have heard the statement, "Live for an audience of One." For Christians it means to fix your eyes on Jesus and live for His glory and purposes—to **seek first the kingdom of God.** That means your first concern in all matters is whether or not your choice and actions merit God's approval, not man's.

- Can you think of some everyday ways your life can demonstrate righteousness? Consider some of the small, often overlooked actions, as well as the big choices that come together to build a reputation of integrity.

- The pursuit of godliness requires discipline. You **will** have to choose against your flesh. But God's grace in Christ is sufficient to help you make those choices if you choose. Ask yourself, do you believe that in Christ you actually have the power to make those hard choices?

▸ What action could you take this week that would cultivate godliness in your life? This isn't a time when you're choosing against an ungodly choice, necessarily, but an action you pursue that builds you up in godliness.

# THE PURSUIT OF FAITH AND LOVE

> But you, O man of God, flee these things and **pursue** righteousness, godliness, **faith, love,** patience, gentleness.
>
> 1 Timothy 6:11 (emphasis mine)

We discussed in chapter five how love has already been placed in the heart of the believer. The same is true of faith. Concerning members of the body of Christ, the apostle Paul declares in Romans 12:3, "God has dealt to each one a measure of faith."

Be that as it may, that measure of faith must be developed by hearing and using it. Romans 10:17 teaches us, "Faith comes by hearing, and hearing by the word of God." God's Word is the food that our faith must feed upon.

Body builders eat a protein rich diet, which when digested becomes the raw material that builds muscle mass. When God's Word is heard and digested through meditation, it produces the raw material that builds faith. To pursue faith, we must pursue God's Word. Do you have a faith problem? Do you find it difficult to believe the promises of God and trust Him completely? More than likely, it has to do with your spiritual diet. It is not possible to be strong in faith while neglecting time in God's book.

Just like you eat regularly in order to use the physical strength that food provides, you must feed regularly upon the promises of God in order to utilize the strength that faith provides. You are not going to derive the strength of faith from a promise that you have a fleeting memory of and haven't read or reflected upon recently any more than you will derive fresh physical strength from a meal you ate weeks ago. You may remember the smell, taste, color, and texture of the food, but you will not gain any physical benefit from a meal eaten in the distant past. Even as the Israelites had to collect fresh manna daily, in order to be people of faith, we need to go back to the Word **daily.** The apostle Paul said that it is with the heart, or the inward man, that we believe and that the inward man is renewed **day by day** (Romans 10:10; 2 Corinthians 4:16; 1 Peter 3:4).

## Feed Your Faith and *Use* It

I know a guy who read all about muscle building techniques—the best foods to eat and the best exercises to do in order to gain strength and build muscles. He even invested in an in-home personal weight training system complete with every gadget and free weight necessary to become the next Mr. Universe. He worked at it faithfully... for two days and then never touched it again. Obviously, his physique never changed.

Faith is like a muscle that must be exercised. The very next verse in 1 Timothy 6—right after where we are told to pursue faith—says, "Fight the good fight of faith" (v. 12). Faith is made for conflict! It grows as it holds onto God's promises and refuses to let go, especially in hard times.

Fighting the good fight of faith is when you choose to trust God in the midst of the storm, when circumstances rise up and tell you that you won't make it and trials assail you on every side. It is when you cling to the promise despite how you feel, regardless of popular opinion, and no matter what the devil might be whispering in your ear. It's not called a "fight" for nothing.

It is where we learn, like the apostle Paul, to stand in the midst of a great storm where others have completely lost hope and say, "Therefore take heart, men, for I believe God that it will be just as it was told me" (Acts 27:25).

Hebrews 11:1 declares, "Now faith is being sure of what we hope for and certain of what we do not see" (NIV 1984). So, fighting the good fight of faith is literally fighting the good fight of being sure of what we hope for and certain of what we do not see. The only thing that will hold us steady when doubts assail us and when things don't seem like they have any possibility of working out are the promises. In fact, without God's Word for something there is no basis for faith. Faith begins at the known will of God and the promises in His Word are a revelation of His will. He has never promised anything that is not His will to perform, and without a promise there is no possibility of faith.

## The Author and Finisher of Our Faith

Hebrews 12:2 refers to Jesus as the author and finisher of our faith. Our faith comes from hearing the Word and it is strengthened by using it, but it is **in** a person: Jesus. Since He is the embodiment of the Word (John 1:14), Jesus is the source of our faith and the greatest teacher of faith who ever lived. As He taught about faith, He designated several different levels, or kinds, of faith. Looking at them will help you identify where you are right now in your faith development so you can see where you need to go in your ongoing pursuit of faith.

## NO FAITH

> On the same day, when evening had come, He said to them, "Let us cross over to the other side." Now when they had left the multitude, they took Him along in the boat as He was. And other little boats were also with Him. And a great windstorm arose, and the waves beat into the boat so that it was already filling. But He was in the stern, asleep on a pillow. And they awoke Him and said to Him, "Teacher, do You not care that we are perishing?"
>
> Then He arose and rebuked the wind and said to the sea, "Peace, be still!" And the wind ceased and there was a great calm. But He said to them, "Why are you so fearful? How is it that you have **no faith?**" (Mark 4:35–40, emphasis mine)

When in jeopardy, the disciples said, "Don't you care?" This represented no faith on their part. They had the Lord's word that they were going to the other side, but when things went wrong His promise meant nothing to them.

The person with no faith accuses God of not caring. "I'm in trouble and God couldn't care less. He is unconcerned for me," they say. If this sounds like you, then I encourage you to press on in your pursuit of faith and discover what happens when you finally begin to take God at His Word.

## LITTLE FAITH

> "Therefore I say to you, **do not worry** about your life, what you will eat or what you will drink; nor about your body, what you will put on. Is not life more than food and the body more than clothing? Look at the birds of the air, for they neither sow nor reap nor gather into barns; yet your heavenly Father feeds them. Are you not of more value than they? Which of you by worrying can add one cubit to his stature?
> 
> "So **why do you worry** about clothing? Consider the lilies of the field, how they grow: they neither toil nor spin; and yet I say to you that even Solomon in all his glory was not arrayed like one of these. Now if God so clothes the grass of the field, which today is, and tomorrow is thrown into the oven, will He not much more clothe you, **O you of little faith?**
> 
> "Therefore **do not worry,** saying, 'What shall we eat?' or 'What shall we drink?' or 'What shall we wear?' For after all these things the Gentiles seek.

> For your heavenly Father knows that you need all these things. But seek first the kingdom of God and His righteousness, and all these things shall be added to you. Therefore **do not worry** about tomorrow, for tomorrow will worry about its own things. Sufficient for the day is its own trouble." (Matthew 6:25–34, emphasis mine)

"Little faith" is riddled with worry and pre-occupied with lack more than with God and His kingdom. In verse 25, Jesus said, **"Do not worry."** In verse 28, He asked, **"Why do you worry?"** In verse 31, He said, **"Do not worry."** And again, in verse 34, He said, **"Do not worry."** Do you think He is trying to get a point across?

Little faith may start out well, but it usually gets strangled by the cares and anxieties of life. The cure is to become more occupied with thoughts of God, His faithfulness, and His ability. We can look to His faithfulness to meet the needs of His creation: the birds and the lilies. We can and certainly **must** look to His Word to see the amazing record of His faithfulness throughout history to those who love and serve Him. That will awaken our faith and help it remain strong in the storms of life.

And we need to be occupied with bigger things than just our own personal needs. The promise is that when you put His kingdom first, all the temporal things that you are tempted to worry about will be added to you. Make it your aim to move from little faith, which is plagued with worries, to great faith.

## GREAT FAITH

> Now when Jesus had entered Capernaum, a centurion came to Him, pleading with Him, saying, "Lord, my servant is lying at home paralyzed, dreadfully tormented."
>
> And Jesus said to him, "I will come and heal him."
>
> The centurion answered and said, "Lord, I am not worthy that You should come under my roof. But only speak a word, and my servant will be healed. For I also am a man under authority, having soldiers under me. And I say to this one, 'Go,' and he goes; and to another, 'Come,' and he comes; and to my servant, 'Do this,' and he does it."
>
> When Jesus heard it, He marveled, and said to those who followed, "Assuredly, I say to you, I have not found such **great faith,** not even in Israel!" (Matthew 8:5–10, emphasis mine)

Though there are several things that could be said about great faith, the most outstanding feature in this story is that it rests on the evidence of the Lord's word alone. **"Only speak a word,** and my servant will be healed" (v. 8). The centurion required no other evidence. The word of Jesus was enough.

When we are faced with adversity—or any kind of crisis—we should look to God's Word as our first line of defense rather than our last-ditch effort. Once you find a promise that covers your need, take it to the Lord in prayer and then thank Him for bringing it to pass, requiring no other evidence beyond the fact that He said it. As one old timer put it: "God said it, I believe it, and that settles it."

We should make it our aim to move from **no faith** to **little faith** to **great faith.** And the best way to do that is to draw close to the author and finisher of our faith, Jesus.

## Faith Works by Love

As I said in chapter five, a very large book could be written on the subject of love alone, but once again I would like to deal with it in its setting as we find it in 1 Timothy 6:11. In this verse, it is linked together with faith. Galatians 5:6 proclaims, "For in Christ Jesus neither circumcision nor uncircumcision avails anything, but faith working through love." Faith works **through** love. Without love, faith has nothing to work through. In the original language, it states that faith is made effectual or active through love. They are an inseparable pair.

In fact, we find faith and love mentioned together so often in the same verse throughout the New Testament that it is almost impossible to miss the significance. Consider these instances:

> 1 Corinthians 13:2, 13 • 2 Corinthians 8:7
> Galatians 5:6 • Ephesians 1:15; 3:17; 6:23
> Colossians 1:4 • 1 Thessalonians 1:3; 3:6; 5:8
> 2 Thessalonians 1:3 • 1 Timothy 1:14; 2:15; 4:12
> 2 Timothy 1:13; 2:22; 3:10 • Titus 2:2; 3:15
> Philemon 5 • James 2:5 • Revelation 2:19

In case you didn't count, that is twenty-three times!

Even as a lack of intake of the Word will starve faith, a lack of love will smother faith. Generally, if it's not a lack of the Word causing a faith problem. It will be a deficiency in the love department. Jesus Himself cited this as the premiere reason for unanswered prayer. Faith makes prayer work, but a lack of love will stifle faith before it ever gets off the ground.

## Whenever You Stand Praying

So Jesus answered and said to them, "Have faith in God. For assuredly, I say to you, whoever says to this mountain, 'Be removed and be cast into the sea,' and does not doubt in his heart, but believes that those things he says will be done, he will have whatever he says. Therefore I say to you, whatever things you ask when you pray, believe that you receive them, and you will have them.

"And whenever you stand praying, if you have anything against anyone, forgive him, that your Father in heaven may also forgive you your trespasses. But if you do not forgive, neither will your Father in heaven forgive your trespasses." (Mark 11:22–26)

Here, where Jesus teaches us so clearly how faith in God works, especially in connection with prayer, He says that if we believe that we receive the things we ask for when we pray, we will have them. The Amplified Bible Classic Edition puts it this way: "Whatever you ask for in prayer, believe (trust and be confident) that it is granted to you, and you will [get it]" (Mark 11:24). We must believe that God hears us and grants our request **when we pray,** not when things begin to look different or when we begin to feel different.

But there is something else we must do when we stand praying: **we must forgive.** And Jesus didn't leave any loopholes. He said we need to forgive if we have **anything** against **anyone!** In order for faith in God to be effective, there must be an exercise of love between people.

### *The Sound of Twigs Breaking*

Many years ago, one of the elders of our church was called upon to visit and pray for a woman that had been bound to a wheelchair for decades due to crippling arthritis. As he laid his hand upon her head to pray, he suddenly drew back, sensing a definite inward hesitation from the Holy Spirit to pray. He told himself that he was probably imagining things and proceeded again to pray. Once again, he felt the Holy Spirit stop him, but this time he had an added impression in his heart: "She needs to forgive," the Spirit seemed to be saying.

"Ma'am, I'm sorry, but I can't pray for you just yet. Are you holding unforgiveness in your heart toward anyone?" he asked. She bowed her head and said, "Yes, I have held bitterness toward my sister for thirty years." He responded, "Well, until you get that taken care of, my prayers won't help you."

Without looking up, she began to pray from her heart, forgiving her sister. Suddenly, there was a sound like dry twigs breaking, as her gnarled, twisted hands and feet began to straighten out. Within moments she was healed, and for the first time in many years, she stood. It was an emotional moment to say the least. I can still remember to this day as that elder described the popping, snapping sound and her miraculous sudden healing. It was a lesson on the power of love and forgiveness that I have never forgotten!

In our walk with Christ it's hard to get any more basic than faith and love. These are foundational and fundamental to every aspect of our ongoing journey with God. Like a garden, they must be nourished and tended to. If we neglect the garden it gets overgrown with weeds, and the plants that we want to bear good fruit will begin to wither. If we want to partake of the good harvest that faith and love bring, we must make their strengthening and growth a main pursuit of our lives.

# A PLAN FOR PURSUIT

For we walk by faith, not by sight.

2 Corinthians 5:7

Thoughts, prayers, and questions to help you make a plan for pursuing faith and love:

- Today's culture views faith as positive, fuzzy feelings that things will work out. How does biblical faith differ from this worldly view?
- In Matthew 28:20, Jesus says, "And lo, I am with you always, even to the end of the age." That is a promise centered in Jesus that you can have faith in. What does it look like to have faith in Christ to follow through on this promise? How might that faith affect your attitude in day-to-day life?
- Why do you think faith and love are so interconnected? How does faith operate through love? Try to be specific and personalize it to your own life.
- Are you struggling to exercise faith in God for a trial or difficulty in your life? Consider whether or not there might be some unforgiveness in your heart that you're holding onto. This may be acting as an obstacle to faith.

Take it before the Lord, confess it (if need be, confess it to the one you've sinned against), and let God empower you to say yes to Him and His promises to you.

# THE PURSUIT OF PATIENCE AND GENTLENESS

We now come to the final two things in 1 Timothy 6:11 that we are told to pursue: **patience** and **gentleness**. And if Timothy, being called a man of God, was told to pursue these things, we would be fooling ourselves to think they would be somehow automatically incorporated into our lives without pursuit on our part. Let's begin with patience.

When it comes to pursuing patience, there are three basic areas that it can be applied to: **promises, people,** and **persecution.** I will deal with each of these in order.

## Promises

We ended the last chapter by talking about how faith works through love. It also works by patience. In the New Testament, we find—just as with love—patience listed in the same verse as faith, again and again. Of the many references where that can be found, at least four times, faith, love, and patience are found bundled together in the same verse (1 Thessalonians 1:3; 1 Timothy 6:11; 2 Timothy 2:2; Revelation 2:19). They are the three cooperating powers when it comes to standing on the promises of God. If you take any one of them away, any desired results from prayer will be greatly undermined.

> And we desire that each one of you show the same diligence to the full assurance of hope until the end, that you do not become sluggish but imitate those who through faith and patience inherit the promises. For when God made a promise to Abraham, because He could swear by no one greater, He swore by Himself, saying, "Surely blessing I will bless you, and multiplying I will multiply you." And so, after he had patiently endured, he obtained the promise. (Hebrews 6:11–15)

The promises are obtained through faith and patience. Abraham and Sarah waited twenty-five years before they experienced the fulfillment of the promised child, Isaac. Though God is absolutely faithful, His timetable is not always in sync with ours. He alone sees every cause, reaction, and result that occurs, both present and future. So in His wisdom, God "does everything at just the right time" (Ecclesiastes 3:11 ERV). That is why patience is required on our part.

Biblical patience has been rightly described as "a brave and enduring perseverance." It is the long-lasting quality of our faith. Its necessity is revealed again in Hebrews 10:36 where we're told, "You have need of endurance, so that after you have done the will of God, you may receive the promise."

Cottonwood Church, which my wife and I founded together, has experienced steady growth throughout the years. From holding services in a small storefront, expanding into a commercial office building, and eventually constructing our first facility that at one time hosted seven services each weekend, it's been an amazing journey.

During those seasons of growth, people would come and see the packed services or the lines of people waiting to get in and say, "Oh my, God has really blessed you!" We would agree, but most of those people didn't have any idea about the trials we went through or the miracles it took to get there. They aren't aware of all the delays, opposition, and tearful prayers. They didn't see the points where we endured in our faith when it seemed impossible for the next step in our journey to happen.

## Lawsuits and Rain

Eventually, we built our present campus, which stands on over thirty acres just a few miles down the road from Disneyland in California. It is an expansive place with multiple buildings, including several auditoriums, the largest of which seats well over three thousand. God has truly blessed us.

But the blessing hasn't come without enduring great battles and without great patience. In fact, from the time we first became engaged in negotiations for property on the street we're on, it was nine years before we finally moved in.

We were sued by two cities, we were locked out of our property due to an attempt to seize it through eminent domain, and for years we were involved in a very difficult and expensive legal battle. For the most part, the media was very unkind and unfair to us, and from a natural standpoint, it looked like the church had no chance.

Eventually, we won in court and could begin to build, but almost every dollar we'd set aside had gone to legal expenses, and now we were faced with trying to get building permits from the same people who had sued us! But God be praised, He worked a miracle that doubled our property and paid for all of our legal costs! We got our plans approved, received the necessary permits . . . and then it began to rain.

It rained and rained and rained. It was the biggest downpour our area had experienced in one hundred years! Our property turned into a lake that we dubbed "Lake Cottonwood." I even went out on it in a canoe to film some video announcements! We had machinery that pumped 2,000 gallons a minute off of the property that ran twenty-four hours a day for two weeks. After most of the water was drained, we were left with a giant muddy field that no building equipment could go on for more than three months until it had sufficiently dried out.

Every promise that God had whispered to my heart came to pass, but not without a huge amount of patience thrown in. If things are taking longer than you hoped or expected, let me encourage you: God and His promises can be relied upon, but it is through faith and patience that you will inherit those promises.

# People

The next area where it is incredibly important to exercise and pursue patience is with people. We must be patient with people as we make allowances for them to change and grow. Ephesians 4:1–2 in the Amplified Bible Classic Edition says, "I therefore, the prisoner for the Lord, appeal to and beg you to walk (lead a life) worthy of the [divine] calling to which you have been called [with behavior that is a credit to the summons to God's service, living as becomes you] with complete lowliness of mind (humility) and meekness (unselfishness, gentleness, mildness), with patience, bearing with one another and making allowances because you love one another."

Some people are so intolerant and impatient with others. It seems like they have forgotten where they themselves came from and how long it took God to get them there. We need to give people room to grow, and as Scripture implores us, to bear with them and make allowances for them while they do. Granted, there will always be someone that just isn't interested in changing or growing at all, but most people are trying.

### *You Need to Do Something About Her!*

Some years ago, a lady in our church came to me absolutely irate over the way a young woman was provocatively dressed in one of our services. "You need to do something about her!" she sternly told me. The young woman she was so upset about had been saved all of three weeks. "I'm going to leave her alone and so are you," I told her. "We're going to let God deal with her." I'd hate to think what that lady would have said if she'd found out that the girl was still living with her boyfriend (which changed, along with her style of dress as she continued to come to church and sit under the teaching of the Word)!

Those who tend to be so harsh and rigid when it comes to making others "toe the line" have somehow lost touch with their own spiritual journey. Most of us were incredibly carnal when we got saved. I know for me personally, I had almost no knowledge of biblical standards, having never been taught the Bible before I was a Christian. It was only as I began to attend church and read the Bible that I realized some of the things that were normal to me and my friends were outside of the boundaries that God had set for Christian behavior.

I do not mean to make an excuse for sinful living, but I do mean to underscore the need for patience with people as they grow in the Lord. Things that were easy for one person to change might be much more difficult in another person's situation depending on their background, the amount of good teaching they have received, and upon the length of time they have been walking with the Lord. We are never using a just balance when we judge others by their worst actions while judging ourselves by our best intentions. A good rule is to always treat others with the same patience and understanding that we would like to receive ourselves.

## Persecution

The third area where we need to pursue patience is when we are persecuted or when we suffer for doing right and living right—and it looks like there is no short-term reward in sight. First Peter 2:19–20 declares, "For this is commendable, if because of conscience toward God one endures grief, suffering wrongfully. For what credit is it if, when you are beaten for your faults, you take it patiently? But when you do good and suffer, if you take it patiently, this is commendable before God."

Sometimes when you obey your conscience and do what is right before God, you will suffer for it. That persecution or ill treatment may come from an employer, the government, or possibly, even from your own family.

I performed a wedding for a couple once where the woman had come out of a major world religion. Her life had been empty and she found glorious fulfillment and purpose when she embraced Christ as Savior. She and her husband-to-be, who was from a similar background, decided that they would have a Christian wedding, refusing to participate in the usual ceremonies that were practiced in her previous religion.

Her family was furious with her, but she was firm. "Pastor, in good conscience we cannot have those ceremonies in our wedding because they have to do with the evil spirits that our old religion worships," she told me. They did what was right before God, but in the process her father disowned her. She was brokenhearted but committed her situation into the hands of God, which is exactly what we are commanded to do.

The very next verses in 1 Peter 2 tell us, "For to this you were called, because Christ also suffered for us, leaving us an example, that you should follow His steps: 'Who committed no sin, nor was deceit found in His mouth'; who, when He was reviled, did not revile in return; when He suffered, He did not threaten, but committed Himself to Him who judges righteously" (vv. 21–23). When He suffered, Jesus committed Himself into the Father's hands, or as The Message Bible puts it, He "was content to let God set things right."

That brokenhearted newlywed and her husband were rewarded by God for their stand. Though they initially suffered for choosing to do the right thing, it wasn't long before her father had a change of heart and welcomed her back into his heart and the family. I don't know if he ever came to Christ, but I believe his daughter's courage and patience paved the way for that to happen.

## God Sees from a Different Perspective

It is marvelous when our patience under persecution pays off quickly, but that is not always the case. God sees things from a different perspective than we do, and much of His reward for our faithfulness will be experienced in eternity. Looking for all of our reward in this life not only reveals ignorance of the Scriptures but is also very shortsighted.

Paul writes to the Romans that God will "'render to each one [that's you, me, and everybody] according to his deeds': eternal life to those who by patient continuance in doing good seek for glory, honor, and immortality" (Romans 2:6-7).

To the Corinthians he writes, "For our light affliction, which is but for a moment, is working for us a far more exceeding and eternal weight of glory" (2 Corinthians 4:17).

To the Thessalonians he says, "So that we ourselves boast of you among the churches of God for your patience and faith in all your persecutions and tribulations that you endure, which is manifest evidence of the righteous judgment of God, that you may be counted worthy of the kingdom of God, for which you also suffer" (2 Thessalonians 1:4–5).

Believers in the early church not only saw mighty miracles of deliverance and favor as they preached the gospel and lived for Christ in their day, they also had a keen awareness that the rewards of God would be experienced largely in the world to come.

### *Chloe*

"The blows seemed to come from everywhere, and Chloe tried to wrap his arms around his head to protect himself. Although he didn't know how many attackers there were, he felt the sharp thud of each blow as he lost consciousness. His attackers shouted at him, mocking his faith and his Jesus. Chloe prayed, silently crying out to God to give him strength.

Each week, Chloe walks more than twenty miles in his native Ivory Coast to preach in a village called Sepikaha. A small group of Christians welcomes Chloe, but the vast majority of the village is Muslim. Those that were radical, militant Muslims were the ones who were beating the preacher.

Chloe was taken to a hospital where his many wounds were treated. When police asked Chloe who had beaten him, he said he didn't know. Chloe has been blind for many years.

The week after he was released from the hospital, Chloe was back in Sepikaha, risking his life to preach to people that he could not see. His eyes were blind, but Chloe's heart could see clearly. It saw a need for Jesus in the small village, and it saw young Christians hungry to grow in their faith. He returns, week after week, to Sepikaha. The faces that he cannot see now, he will see one day in heaven."[2]

Chloe's physical eyes may have been blind, but the eyes of his heart held heaven and the coming rewards in perfect focus. The world is not worthy of such men.

## The Pursuit of Gentleness

Everyone that serves Christ with all of his or her heart is acquainted with suffering to one degree or another. But not everyone is gentle or kind while they are suffering. Some are like a wild animal caught in a net, striking out at anyone who comes near. In 1 Timothy 6:11, we are told to pursue gentleness right along with patience.

The word translated *gentleness* in this verse could also be rendered "meekness." To the Western mind it almost carries with it the thought of weakness, in that someone would be meek because they are powerless. Vine's Expository Dictionary of New Testament Words declares, "It must be clearly understood, therefore, that the meekness manifested by the Lord and commended to the believer is the fruit of power." The common assumption is that when a man is meek it is because he cannot help himself, but the

---

[2] The Voice of the Martyrs, "The Ivory Coast: Chloe," in *Extreme Devotion: The Voice of the Martyrs* (Nashville: W Publishing Group, 2001), 51.

Lord was meek because He had the infinite resources of God at His command.

Jesus invites us to come to Him and learn about His gentleness and meekness. In Matthew's gospel, He says, "Come to Me, all you who labor and are heavy laden, and I will give you rest. Take My yoke upon you and learn from Me, for I am gentle and lowly in heart, and you will find rest for your souls. For My yoke is easy and My burden is light" (Matthew 11:28–30).

When you begin to learn the secret of Jesus' gentleness, your soul will come into a marvelous rest. Jesus' gentle and humble heart was due to His intimate relationship with the Father (Matthew 11:27), and as you respond to His invitation and begin to spend time with Him, the same eternal work will be wrought in you in ever-increasing measure.

### No Need to Impress

The more time I spend in Christ's presence, the more I realize that He's in charge and that I'm His. That always brings an underlying confidence, which frees me from the need of feeling like I have to impress others. And my soul can be at rest.

The person who is outwardly brash, loud, and arrogant is often inwardly filled with doubt and a lack of confidence. These people are compensating for their inward sense of inadequacy—their world would come crashing down if everyone realized how weak and afraid they actually feel.

I read an article once written by a guy that had been known as a man's man. Wherever he went he always made his presence known through his loud, over-the-top behavior. He always had to drink the most or be the funniest person at a party. He would never back down from a dare and always went the extra mile to impress people. He even shared how at one party he had eaten glass to prove his manliness.

Eventually his world collapsed. He could no longer maintain the façade. It turns out he had been suffering from panic attacks for years and was tormented by irrational fears almost daily. In trying to find help, he finally confessed that all of his bombastic behavior over the years had been his attempt to cover up a huge deficiency in his soul.

My friend, the only cure for such things is to come to Jesus and learn about His gentleness and humility. His Father is our Father, and we are loved just like Jesus is (John 17:23). One of the great rewards of pursuing gentleness is rest for your soul.

## Other Benefits

According to Galatians 5:23, gentleness is a fruit of the Spirit and in 1 Timothy 3:3 it is listed as a qualification for leadership in the Church. As you draw near to Christ and fill your heart with His Word, the fruit of gentleness will grow and begin to be expressed in your life daily. And yes, there are times when a firm hand is required to handle difficult or unyielding people in life—both inside the Church and outside of it—but you will generally get much further by dealing with people in a spirit of gentleness than with harshness.

Second Timothy 2:23–26 illustrates this well: "But avoid foolish and ignorant disputes, knowing that they generate strife. And a servant of the Lord must not quarrel but be gentle to all, able to teach, patient, in humility correcting those who are in opposition, if God perhaps will grant them repentance, so that they may know the truth, and that they may come to their senses and escape the snare of the devil, having been taken captive by him to do his will."

Correcting people in a spirit of humility and gentleness will do infinitely better than quarreling with them. Gentleness disarms people. Many times, it is the only way you can get someone to listen and hopefully come to their senses and repent.

Even when it comes to restoring a brother or sister who has been overtaken in some sin, we are told to do so in a spirit of gentleness. We don't come in with guns blazing on our high horse, denouncing the person for their weakness or condemning them for their entanglement in sin. We don't shoot our wounded. In a spirit of humility, we are to restore them (Galatians 6:1).

At times in his ministry, the apostle Paul was quite stern, like when he publicly opposed Peter over his hypocrisy regarding the works of the law versus grace (Galatians 2:11–21), or with the sorcerer Elymas who sought to turn the proconsul from the faith (Acts 13:6–12). But you cannot read his epistles or the overall exploits of his ministry without sensing a deep spirit of gentleness that permeated most of what he did and said, especially when dealing with those in the Church.

Writing to the Corinthians, he said, "Now I, Paul, myself am pleading with you by the meekness and gentleness of

Christ" (2 Corinthians 10:1). In 1 Thessalonians 2:7–8, he said, "But we were gentle among you, just as a nursing mother cherishes her own children. So, affectionately longing for you, we were well pleased to impart to you not only the gospel of God, but also our own lives, because you had become dear to us."

## Bone-Breaking Influence

Proverbs 25:15 announces to us, "By long forbearance a ruler is persuaded, and a gentle tongue breaks a bone." The Amplified Bible Classic Edition says, "Soft speech breaks down the most bonelike resistance." That truth is echoed in Proverbs 15:1 where it says, "A gentle answer turns away wrath, but harsh words stir up anger" (NLT 1996).

I was naive, I admit it, but I wasn't expecting to be laughed at. I had gone down to City Hall to find out about getting a conditional use permit to hold church services in a commercial office building that we wanted to rent. After telling the secretary the reason for my visit, I was ushered into the city manager's office. He and another city official were seated, talking. "Can I help you?" he asked. "Yes," I said. "I'd like to find out about getting a conditional use permit to have church services in a local building." I told them where it was and that it was currently empty. They looked at each other and then at me and began laughing. "You're wasting your time. It's not going to happen," they told me in so many words. They were arrogant and condescending, and that was pretty much the end of the conversation.

Needless to say, I left a bit deflated. After taking it to God in prayer for several days, I felt like the Lord was telling me to go back and try again. But I had the distinct impression that I was to go in an opposite spirit than the one they had displayed. "Go in a spirit of gentleness and humility," the Lord seemed to say to me. So I did. I didn't come groveling or begging, but I didn't come demanding or threatening either.

The first person that met me was the mayor. I explained to him why I was there and what had occurred on my last visit. He marched me right into the city manager's office and began by asking why I had been laughed at. The city manager immediately apologized. The mayor then said, "I think we can help this man get his permit." At the next city council meeting, our permit was approved and we began holding services almost immediately. That bone-hard resistance was broken down by the power of a gentle response. I went in a spirit of meekness because heaven's resources were at my disposal, not because I felt inferior or afraid.

In breaking down resistance or building up the downcast and fallen, gentleness is essential. It must be something you pursue, until **your gentleness is known to everyone**.

Patience and gentleness. They are easy to talk about, but difficult, at times, to display. As we pursue them, we are inwardly changed. We become more like Jesus, and ultimately, that's God's goal for us believers, isn't it?

# A PLAN FOR PURSUIT

Rest in the Lord, and wait patiently for Him.

Psalm 37:7

Thoughts, prayers, and questions to help you make a plan for pursuing patience and gentleness:

- We discussed how patience can be applied to promises, people, and persecution. Can you think of an example from your own life in each of those categories when patience was required?

- Second Peter 3:9 says, "The Lord is not slack concerning His promise, as some count slackness, but is longsuffering toward us, not willing that any should perish but that all should come to repentance." You see how God demonstrated patience, or "longsuffering," in His gracious dealings with us—and He continues to show that patience to the lost today. How might that affect your own attitude when you're called upon to exercise patience with others?

- Some people confuse gentleness with naiveté. But you wouldn't call Jesus naïve. Consider how Jesus—with matchless power and omniscient insight—often used gentleness with sinners to change hearts from the inside out. How do you think people today would respond if God's people met them in their need with that kind of gentleness?

▸ In a world where people fight tooth and nail to get what they want and think they need, gentleness is disarming because it doesn't try to manipulate people or situations for selfish gain. Try to think of three ways you could show gentleness in your daily life.

# 9

# PURSUING PURPOSE

And behold, a man of God went from Judah to Bethel by the word of the Lord, and Jeroboam stood by the altar to burn incense. Then he cried out against the altar by the word of the Lord, and said, "O altar, altar! Thus says the Lord: 'Behold, a child, Josiah by name, shall be born to the house of David; and on you he shall sacrifice the priests of the high places who burn incense on you, and men's bones shall be burned on you.'"

1 Kings 13:1–2

This remarkable prophecy was given 322 years before Josiah was born! Josiah was only eight years old when he became king. His father, King Amon, and his grandfather, Manasseh, were both incredibly wicked men who worshiped and served idols. Josiah had no godly model or pattern to follow. Yet astonishingly, young Josiah loved God and chose to serve Him.

At this point in the nation of Israel's story, the people had almost completely lost the knowledge of the Lord, and the land had become full of pagan altars and idol worship. But when Josiah was eighteen, one of the priests found a copy of the law when they were carrying out repairs on the temple of the Lord. It was read before young king Josiah and when he heard it, he ripped his clothes and basically said, "We're in trouble!"

From that point on, he goes on a crusade to bring Israel back to God. He has the book of the law read before all of Israel and immediately begins to cleanse the temple of idols. He also goes throughout the land tearing down and destroying every vestige of pagan worship (2 Kings 21–23). Then we come to one of the most amazing occurrences in history.

As Josiah was going through the land destroying idols, we read, "Moreover the altar that was at Bethel, and the high place which Jeroboam the son of Nebat, who made Israel sin, had made, both that altar and the high place he broke down; and he burned the high place and crushed it to powder, and burned the wooden image. As Josiah turned, he saw the tombs that were there on the mountain. And he sent and took the bones out of the tombs and burned them on the altar, and defiled it according to the word of the Lord which the man of God proclaimed, who proclaimed these words. Then he said, 'What gravestone is this that I see?' So the men of the city told him, 'It is the tomb of the man of God who came from Judah and proclaimed these things which you have done against the altar of Bethel'" (2 Kings 23:15–17).

It is absolutely staggering to try and imagine what that moment must have been like for Josiah. To realize that he was standing in the middle of his destiny, that he was living out the purpose that God had created him for and called him to. The reality of the words of Isaiah spoken so many years before had suddenly been emblazoned upon his soul: "Behold, the former things have come to pass, and new things I declare; before they spring forth I tell you of them" (Isaiah 42:9).

## Isaiah's Prophecy of Cyrus

Like the unnamed man of God that prophesied of Josiah's deeds and name, Isaiah made a similar prophecy in his day. In Isaiah 44:28 we read, "Who says of Cyrus, 'He is My shepherd, and he shall perform all My pleasure, saying to Jerusalem, "You shall be built," And to the temple, "Your foundation shall be laid."'" These words may have meant very little to the generation that heard them, but if we move several generations into the future, their impact is shocking.

> Now in the first year of Cyrus king of Persia, that the word of the Lord by the mouth of Jeremiah might be fulfilled, the Lord stirred up the spirit of Cyrus king of Persia, so that he made a proclamation throughout all his kingdom, and also put it in writing, saying, Thus says Cyrus king of Persia: All the kingdoms of the earth the Lord God of heaven has given me. And He has commanded me to build Him a house at Jerusalem which is in Judah. Who is among you of all His people? May the Lord his God be with him, and let him go up! (2 Chronicles 36:22–23)

Jeremiah prophesied that these events would happen after seventy years, which is amazing in its accuracy. But Isaiah, 175 years before Cyrus was born and 213 years before it was fulfilled, foretold not only of the event, but also the name of the one who would do it. Destiny! Purpose unfolding! The plan of God coming to pass through the one He had ordained would do these things.

God told Jeremiah, "Before I formed you in the womb I knew you; before you were born I sanctified you; I ordained you a prophet to the nations" (Jeremiah 1:5). *Well, I wish I had a God-given purpose like that,* you may be thinking. The truth is **you do!** And God's design is that your life and activity should revolve around that purpose.

Ephesians 2:8–10 declares, "For by grace you have been saved through faith, and that not of yourselves; it is the gift of God, not of works, lest anyone should boast. For we are His workmanship, created in Christ Jesus **for good works, which God prepared beforehand that we should walk in them**" (emphasis mine). The Ronald Knox translation puts it this way: "We are his design; God has created us in Christ Jesus, pledged to such good actions as he has prepared beforehand, to be the employment of our lives" (v. 10).

The fact is that God's work with us doesn't stop with salvation. That is only the beginning. He has work for you to do on this earth—good work that He has prepared **beforehand** to be the employment of your life. *Beforehand* refers to before the foundation of the world (Ephesians 1:4). You are not on earth—at this time—by accident. You are not reading these words by accident. God planned for you to be here, and He has a pre-ordained purpose for your life. You count! You have a destiny to fulfill and a purpose to pursue.

## Why He Laid Hold of Me

In Paul's letter to the Philippians, a church with which he had a very special relationship, he speaks about one of the great pursuits of his life. And in so doing, he reveals what should be one of the central pursuits of every follower of Jesus.

He writes, "Not that I have already attained, or am already perfected; but I press on, that I may lay hold of that for which Christ Jesus has also laid hold of me. Brethren, I do not count myself to have apprehended; but one thing I do, forgetting those things which are behind and reaching forward to those things which are ahead, I press toward the goal for the prize of the upward call of God in Christ Jesus" (Philippians 3:12–14).

The phrases *I press on* in verse 12 and *I press toward* in verse 14 are a translation of the same Greek word for "pursue" that we have been studying throughout this book. It is the same word used to command us to pursue peace, the knowledge of God, hospitality, the good of all, love, righteousness, godliness, faith, patience, and gentleness.

What was Paul's great pursuit? What was he trying to lay hold of? **He was pursuing and trying to lay hold of the purpose for which Christ had laid hold of him!** It is a progressive revelation—one that will continually unfold throughout your lifetime—and no one ever fully arrives, but you can discern and lay hold of God's purpose for and in you during the particular season that you are in. And there is a prize waiting in heaven for those that press in and pursue the purpose of God for their lives.

## Why Should We Pursue God's Purpose for Our Lives?

"Why is it so important that I pursue and fulfill God's purpose for my life?" you may ask. Let me give you three reasons.

## REASON 1: You will be bored if you don't.

There will be an emptiness in your life if you don't chase after all God has for you. It's an emptiness that cannot be filled with any other thing. It is an emptiness that even salvation cannot fill. Our churches are teeming with people who are saved, yet they still live without a specific purpose.

They certainly can share Christ with others and they should. They can serve in God's house and they should, but there is still a deep emptiness that gnaws at many people because they haven't found their particular lane yet. They may be doing things that are good—perhaps even noble—but they have yet to find that thing or those things that God has uniquely created them to do: those good works prepared beforehand that they are to be involved in as the employment of their lives. Jesus has laid hold of them, but they haven't laid hold of the "why."

The answer to that question only comes through pursuit. And God is not hiding the answer from us. He wants us to know. Ephesians 5:17 says, "Therefore do not be unwise, but understand what the will of the Lord is." Join the pursuit!

Don't trade in life's great adventure for the security of a predictable and sedate lifestyle. God wants you to live—really live—but the kind of living to the fullest God has in mind for you will only be discovered as you seek Him and begin to lay hold of the specific "why" you are here. As one of my friends often says, "You were born an original, it would be a tragedy if you died as a copy."

There is no doubt that as God begins to reveal His purpose for you—or perhaps we could say, how you fit into His purpose—there will be challenges and risks involved. But we were made for that. No one was created to live a stale, colorless, tame, boring life. We were created in a unique way, with accompanying gifts to serve in God's kingdom. And the Creator—the One who sang creation into existence, the One who spans the heavens with the palm of His hand and who will one day roll it up like a scroll—is not boring! To walk with Him and work with Him is the greatest adventure imaginable and well worth the ongoing pursuit that gets us into the groove for whatever season we are in.

## REASON 2: Because you will never be the blessing to others that God intends you to be if you are not flowing in your purpose.

Consider what God said to Abraham in Genesis 12:1-3: "Now the Lord had said to Abram: 'Get out of your country, from your family and from your father's house, to a land that I will show you. I will make you a great nation; I will bless you and make your name great; and you shall be a blessing. I will bless those who bless you, and I will curse him who curses you; and in you all the families of the earth shall be blessed.'"

Abraham's potential to be a blessing was tied to him being in God's plan and purpose. He only became a great blessing because he followed God's great calling. Was there risk involved? Yes! Did he have to walk by faith? Yes! He left the comfortable and the predictable and by faith walked into history and became a blessing to the whole world!

"But I'm too old to start thinking about change and venturing out by faith," some will say. Abraham was seventy-five when God spoke to him, and he began his journey of faith (Genesis 12:4)!

I know two men who were in their sixties when they packed up and moved to new locations to begin a fresh chapter of ministry. Both were told by friends and leading members of their denominations that they were crazy. "You're too old to start in a new place. You will be leaving family and friends. It doesn't make any sense," they were told.

But each man had a deep conviction that the stream of God's purpose for this season in their life was drawing them to new locations—one to a different state and the other to an entirely new country! In the next two decades, both men experienced blessing and influence that they had never known before. And quite literally, they both have had a measurable impact on world evangelism.

And it's important to make clear that it's not about personal financial gain. That may be involved, but the focus is finding fulfillment, obeying God, and being a blessing—things that you can't put a price on.

There was a man in our church who held a very good job that rewarded him financially more than adequately, but he was not content. He had begun seeking God about his role in the kingdom and had the distinct impression that he was made for something other than his present employment.

"What's in your heart?" I asked him. "I feel like God has created me to coach basketball," he said. After much prayer and discussion with his wife, he applied at several schools for a coaching job, and before long he ended up leaving his job to accept a position as a high school athletic director and basketball coach. The last time I spoke with him, he was brimming with excitement. He was having a great influence in the lives of a number of young men and other coaches and was having a winning season to boot! His pay was less than his previous job, but his joy and kingdom influence had gone into overdrive.

## REASON 3: Because we only get rewarded for doing what God has called us to do.

Commenting on Philippians 3:14 where Paul exclaims, **"I press toward the mark"** or more literally, **"I pursue along the line,"** Adam Clarke writes:

> This is a reference to the white line that marked the ground in the stadium, from the starting place to the goal, on which the runners were obliged to keep their eye fixed; for they who transgressed or went beyond this line did not run lawfully, and were not crowned, even though they got first to the goal.

If we are going to receive the prize or be otherwise rewarded, we must stay in our own lane. It is never wise to compare yourself with or compete with others (2 Corinthians 10:12). Their gifting and calling are as unique as yours. We are all made differently and though you may find inspiration from others and learn from what they have done or are doing, you need to pursue and discover your own unique purpose in the kingdom.

Have you ever noticed what a long-distance runner looks like compared to a sprinter? Or what the physique of a shot putter looks like compared to that of someone who competes in the javelin throw? They are vastly different. Both of the runners run and both the shot putter and javelin thrower throw something, but their individual, physical gifting makes them well fitted for their particular event—not for all events, even those that may have similarities to their own.

Notice Paul's language as he talks about God's purpose for him: "But none of these things move me; nor do I count my life dear to myself, so that I may finish **my race** with joy, and **the ministry which I received from the Lord Jesus,** to testify to the gospel of the grace of God" (Acts 20:24, emphasis mine). Paul knew what **his** race was and he knew what he had personally received from the Lord.

In John 17:4, Jesus prayed to the Father and said, "I have glorified You on the earth. I have finished the work which You have given Me to do." You have a race to run. You have a work to do. Before the foundation of the world, God knew you and planned for you to be here—at this time in history. Satisfaction and fulfillment come as you discover and begin to do those things for which you were created. God did not leave you out when He made His plans. You do have a part. You are gifted. And you can make a difference.

## Where Do I Start?

First of all, **don't panic!** I realize that for some, these thoughts are quite new. They may have never truly considered that they have a unique role to play in God's master plan. And they certainly don't want to miss out on the blessing they could be to others or on the reward associated with finishing their race. But they think, "But so much time has already gone by! What if the things I'm doing now are not what God has for me?"

Paul gives excellent advice for these kinds of questions when he says, "Everyone should remain after God calls him in the station or condition of life in which the summons found him" (1 Corinthians 7:20 AMPC). The Living Bible puts it this way, "Usually a person should keep on with the work he was doing when God called him." If you were a grocer when you got saved, stay with it. Are you a secretary? A student? A dentist? A brick layer? Stay with it. Serve God where you are. Bloom where you're planted but begin to pray and seek God for the next step He wants you to take.

You may be able to completely fulfill God's calling for your life from the context of your present employment. Or, perhaps, God will have other things for you. Pursue Him. Pursue your purpose as it relates to His plans. All you are responsible for is to listen and obey (John 10:27).

God rarely gives us His entire plan for our lives. He gives us a step. And as we faithfully take that step, then He gives us the next. Psalm 37:23 says, "The **steps** of a good man are ordered by the Lord, and He delights in his way." Psalm 40:2 says, He "set my feet on a rock and established my **steps**." Psalm 119:133 says, "Direct my **steps** by Your word." Proverbs 16:9 says, "A man's heart plans his way, but the Lord directs his **steps**" (emphasis in each verse mine).

You don't need to be concerned for your whole journey of faith. Just for the step right in front of you. Perhaps you might consider taking a moment now to seek the Lord. Dare to ask Him what His next step is for your life. Even if the impression the Holy Spirit gives you is small, it always pays to obey, and when we are faithful in the small, He entrusts us with larger things.

## Questions to Get You Started

I want to share with you some questions that I have found helpful in my own journey. Your answers to these questions should be earnestly prayed about and placed before the Lord as you seek His direction and purpose for your life.

## QUESTION 1: What grieves your heart?

In Job 30:25, Job asks, "Has not my soul grieved for the poor?" As you read his story it becomes clear that part of his calling and purpose was to be a helper to the poor. David was grieved over Goliath's taunts and determined that if no one else would do anything about it, he would. His purpose was to be a leader and a warrior.

In Acts 17:16 we read, "Now while Paul waited for them at Athens, his spirit was provoked within him when he saw that the city was given over to idols." The word *provoked* means "to be deeply troubled or grieved." The next verse begins with "Therefore." When we are grieved or troubled in our spirits about something, there should always be a "therefore." God generally gifts us to fix or influence for good the things that make us mad. The thing that grieves your heart can be a powerful signpost pointing you toward your purpose.

Paul was deeply grieved in his spirit when he saw the wholesale worship of idols in the city of Athens. "Therefore he reasoned in the synagogue with the Jews and with the Gentile worshipers, and in the marketplace daily with those who happened to be there" (Acts 17:17).

I used to listen to a particular early morning talk show on Christian radio that I found fascinating. Almost every morning they had an interview with someone that was impacting his or her local neighborhood or society in general. There were people who had invented new health products, people who had devised plans to eradicate illiteracy in their community, and people who had written books on managing money, as well as a host of other positive things.

And almost without fail, at the core of their decision to pursue the thing they had created or done was an anger or an inward grief over something that had happened in their lives or that they had observed in the lives of others. One man who had developed a health food line had lost both of his parents to obesity-related illnesses. A woman who had developed a youth community program got tired of seeing so many young men in her neighborhood end up in jail. A man who had written a book on managing finances talked about how it angered him to see people strangled by poverty when there was a way out.

What makes you mad? What provokes you in your spirit? What grieves your heart? As you prayerfully answer this, don't say, "Why doesn't someone do something about this?" More than likely, God is calling you to get involved and be part of the solution.

## QUESTION 2: What makes you come alive?

Gil Bailie attributes this noteworthy quote to Howard Thurman: "Don't ask yourself what the world needs. Ask yourself what makes you come alive and then go do that. Because what the world needs is people who have come alive."

What do you love to do, or what did you used to love to do before you buried your heart's dreams? I believe that God gives us the grace to enjoy whatever He calls us to do. In Acts 20:24, where Paul talked about his race and the ministry he had received from the Lord, he talked about finishing his race with joy. Certainly, there are hardships and difficult things to navigate along God's pathway of purpose, but one of the overall, outstanding features that earmark the calling God has for us is joy. If what you're doing with your life brings you no joy, then perhaps it's time to reassess the pathway you have chosen.

Many years ago, I spent the day with some friends in a remote area on the west coast of Australia. We had the privilege of meeting and speaking at length with an elderly man who had spent his life as a park ranger of sorts for that region. He knew every insect and animal, every bush and every tree in the area, and as he described them—their purpose and their habits—it was almost like we had stepped into a gravitational field. He spoke with such obvious passion and enthusiasm that we were automatically pulled into his world. It was fascinating! He had found his niche and was living in his purpose. He had found the thing that made him come alive.

What about you? Are you—or were you—most alive with an empty canvas before you and a pallet of paints and brushes in hand? Or sitting with an unformed lump of clay on the potter's wheel? Or sitting in the seat of a plane? Or at a computer getting ready to write another short story? Or working with kids? What makes you come alive?

And just to be clear, I am not advocating that you quit your job and launch out on a new career path—at least not without much prayer and counsel. But I am suggesting that you honestly and courageously answer the question of where your passion is and seek God for His direction. Life is too short to spend it running in the wrong lane.

## QUESTION 3: What are you naturally good at?

I think that many people, even before they are saved, have naturally gravitated toward their God-given gifting and calling. Consider the apostle Paul. Before he became a Christian, he was a religious scholar who had dedicated his life to God. Why hadn't he ended up in politics or as an artist? I believe that he had stumbled upon his purpose, even before he met Christ.

Think of Moses, who at forty years of age had it come into his heart to visit the children of Israel. He attempted to be a deliverer and a judge for them even before he had an encounter with or a calling from God (Acts 7:23–29). Again, even before he knew God, he had intuitively picked up on his purpose. Perhaps that is your story as well. It is not always the case, but many times I have found that it is. As long as I can remember, I always ended up being the leader of whatever I did. Whether I was hiking through the woods with friends or building a fort with kids from the neighborhood, I always ended up taking the lead. I believe that it had to do with my purpose and gifting in life and that ultimately God would use me to lead Cottonwood Church and several other ministry endeavors.

One important thing to keep in mind as you pursue your purpose is that while it may differ somewhat from season to season, it will always relate back in one way or another to God's great purpose of redemption in Christ. There is nothing more important to God than rescuing and restoring precious men and women to what He intended them to be—men and women who have been made in His image and destined to spend an eternity somewhere.

Ephesians 2:10 declares, "For we are His workmanship, created in Christ Jesus for good works, which God prepared beforehand that we should walk in them." The Greek word translated "workmanship" is *poiema*. It is the root word that the English word *poem* comes from. In other words, our lives are not meant to be without rhyme or reason or to be void of balance or purpose. He has a plan for you. Pursue the next step of purpose He has for your life. Begin living your life by design—His design.

# A PLAN FOR PURSUIT

> And we know that all things work together for good to those who love God, to those who are the called according to His purpose.
>
> Romans 8:28

Thoughts, prayers, and questions to help you make a plan for pursuing purpose:

- When it comes to God's purpose for you, the first thing you must settle in your mind is that **you do have a purpose in God's story.** You have a unique calling from God in which your life will bring Him glory and build His Kingdom.

- Before wading into the specifics of God's call on your life, first invite God into the journey. Tell God that your heart's desire is to live out His purpose for your life. Then ask Him to lead you in the journey of discovering that purpose.

- Take some time to consider the three questions posed in this chapter:

    What grieves your heart?

What makes you come alive?

What are you naturally good at?

- As you pursue God's purpose for your life, consider this counsel: God will not lead you into a purpose that requires you to go against His commands or biblical wisdom.

God's unique purpose for you will always fall in line with His great purpose for all Christians—that we join Him in the work of redemption.

# 10

# PURSUING LOST THINGS

In this final chapter, I want to help you consider a slightly different approach to the subject of pursuit. From one of the early stories in David's life, we will be looking at some vital and very relevant principles that will aid us in the pursuit of recovering lost or stolen things. The story takes place before David was recognized as Israel's king while he was still fleeing from Saul.

> Now it happened, when David and his men came to Ziklag, on the third day, that the Amalekites had invaded the South and Ziklag, attacked Ziklag and burned it with fire, and had taken captive the women and those who were there, from small to great; they did not kill anyone, but carried them away and went their way. So David and his men came to the city, and there it was, burned with fire; and their wives, their sons, and their daughters had been taken captive. Then David and the people who were with him lifted up their voices and wept, until they had no more power to weep. And David's

two wives, Ahinoam the Jezreelitess, and Abigail the widow of Nabal the Carmelite, had been taken captive. Now David was greatly distressed, for the people spoke of stoning him, because the soul of all the people was grieved, every man for his sons and his daughters. But David strengthened himself in the Lord his God.

Then David said to Abiathar the priest, Ahimelech's son, "Please bring the ephod here to me." And Abiathar brought the ephod to David. So David inquired of the Lord, saying, **"Shall I pursue** this troop? Shall I overtake them?"

And He answered him, **"Pursue,** for you shall surely overtake them and without fail recover all."

So David went, he and the six hundred men who were with him, and came to the Brook Besor, where those stayed who were left behind. But **David pursued,** he and four hundred men; for two hundred stayed behind, who were so weary that they could not cross the Brook Besor.

Then they found an Egyptian in the field, and brought him to David; and they gave him bread and he ate, and they let him drink water. And they gave him a piece of a cake of figs and two clusters of raisins. So when he had eaten, his strength came back to him; for he had eaten no bread nor drunk water for three days and three nights. Then David said to him, "To whom do you belong, and where are you from?"

> And he said, "I am a young man from Egypt, servant of an Amalekite; and my master left me behind, because three days ago I fell sick. We made an invasion of the southern area of the Cherethites, in the territory which belongs to Judah, and of the southern area of Caleb; and we burned Ziklag with fire."
>
> And David said to him, "Can you take me down to this troop?"
>
> So he said, "Swear to me by God that you will neither kill me nor deliver me into the hands of my master, and I will take you down to this troop."
>
> And when he had brought him down, there they were, spread out over all the land, eating and drinking and dancing, because of all the great spoil which they had taken from the land of the Philistines and from the land of Judah. Then David attacked them from twilight until the evening of the next day. Not a man of them escaped, except four hundred young men who rode on camels and fled. So David recovered **all** that the Amalekites had carried away, and David rescued his two wives. And **nothing of theirs was lacking**, either small or great, sons or daughters, spoil or anything which they had taken from them; David recovered **all**. (1 Samuel 30:1–19, emphasis mine)

Did you see that? David pursued and recovered **all**—nothing was lost. God is a God of recovery. He recovers lost souls, lost relationships, lost hopes, lost prosperity, and lost health. Perhaps you have lost something in your life or maybe the enemy has stolen something from you. Let me share a number of thoughts from this story that will help you as you pursue recovery.

## THOUGHT 1: Take time to weep.

In verse 4 it says, "Then David and the people who were with him lifted up their voices and wept, until they had no more power to weep." Feeling sorrow or anguish and expressing it is not wrong. It is normal. Especially when you have experienced a sudden, personal loss.

David's family had gone into sudden captivity. Maybe you have children who are backslidden, away from God, or in spiritual captivity. Or perhaps there has been the loss of position or possessions or some other thing of meaning or value to you.

Unfortunately, it has been the experience of some in God's family that have experienced such losses to be harshly challenged or even chastised rather than comforted. The last thing a person grieving a loss needs to hear is, "Where is your faith? What's wrong with you, do you think that God has died or something?" To do that almost denies the fact that we are emotional beings and that loss does affect us on an emotional level.

Some who have lost loved ones to death have, in some cases, been made to feel that if they are Christians, it is wrong to grieve. It is true that when a believer dies, this person gains. The believer has departed to be with Christ, which is far better. But there is still an undeniable loss on the part of his or her loved ones and friends here on earth, and grieving that loss is natural. It may not be like the grief of the unsaved who have no hope of being reunited in heaven, but there is still the sting felt by the absence of that loved one, and tears are likely to be shed for some time over the loss.

It's okay to grieve and to express sorrow and pain over loss, especially sudden loss. Sometimes you just need to open the floodgates and weep until you're done. The Scripture says that David and the people with him wept until they had no more power to weep. Ecclesiastes 3:4 says there is "a time to weep." When we experience the loss of something or someone valuable or close to us is one of those times.

## THOUGHT 2: Don't blame others.

While David along with everyone else was grieving the loss of their families, his men laid the blame at his feet. In verse 6, they even spoke of stoning him! Maybe they were saying, "If we hadn't been raiding the Amalekites, they wouldn't have done this to us! You shouldn't have left our city unguarded! You shouldn't have led us in being gone so long! It's your fault and we're going to stone you!"

Don't be in the group that always has to blame someone else. It won't make you feel any better; it will make them feel worse, and it strains relationships. One of the first corrupt fruits of sin seen moments after Adam and Eve disobeyed in the Garden is the shifting of blame to others. When answering God as to whether he had disobeyed Adam said, "The woman you gave to be with me, she gave me of the tree and I ate" (Genesis 3:12). In other words,

"It's the **woman's** fault, and it's **your** fault for giving her to me!" When Eve was asked the same question, she said, "The serpent deceived me, and I ate" (Genesis 3:13). She immediately shifted the blame to the serpent.

### Don't Blame God

Many people, like Adam and Eve, blame God for their losses. David, however, did not, though it would have been an easy thing for him to do. David had been serving the Lord. It was because of the call of God on his life that he had been a fugitive. If he hadn't honored God in sparing Saul's life, he wouldn't have been in this mess.

He could have shaken his fist at God and said, "How could **You** allow this to happen? I've not been perfect, but You know my heart. I've tried to serve you and do what's right. Do you realize everything I have lost? Do you know what serving you has cost me? And now, the people you've called me to lead want to stone me! Why, God?"

A man shared with me once how both his wife and his daughter were in the hospital at the same time. Both of their lives were hanging by a thread. It was the worst possible situation imaginable. One of the doctors who had worked on both his wife and daughter saw him and noticed the Bible under his arm. As he motioned toward the Bible, the doctor quipped, "That's not working too well for you, is it?" The man could have been angry—or cynical, like that doctor—and blamed God, but he didn't.

We need to realize that we are living in a fallen world and everything doesn't function according to God's original creation plan. Sin has messed things up, the devil has messed things up, and people's selfish choices have messed things up. God sent Jesus to make things right. It starts in the hearts of those who believe and is brought about as they pray and work in cooperation with God, but ultimately, He is going to make all things new, including a new heaven and a new earth where everything is right—inside and out.

Until that day, let us keep in mind the words of Jesus, where He drew a bold delineation between the source of good and evil. In John 10:10 He said, "The thief does not come except to steal, and to kill, and to destroy. I have come that they may have life, and that they may have it more abundantly." If it kills, steals, and destroys, don't blame God. If it brings abundant life, give Him the credit.

## THOUGHT 3: Strengthen yourself.

"David was greatly distressed, for the people spoke of stoning him, because the soul of all the people was grieved, every man for his sons and daughters. **But David strengthened himself in the Lord his God**" (1 Samuel 30:6, emphasis mine). You cannot blame God and strengthen yourself in Him at the same time. It's okay to weep when you suffer loss, but when you're done, you need to strengthen yourself.

It may be through worship that you find strength; it may be through reading His Word, or by reminding yourself how God has spoken to you or helped you in the past, which I personally believe David was doing. I think he was rehearsing God's promises to bring him to the throne and recalling the many times in the past of how God had aided him and delivered him.

The Scriptures reveal a habit of David's that would be a worthwhile acquisition for every believer: **in times of trouble, David would talk to his soul**. In Psalm 42—which Charles Spurgeon declares can have no other author besides David—we read these words in verse 10: "As with a breaking of my bones, my enemies reproach me, while they say to me all day long, 'Where is your God?'" That certainly describes what David must have been going through in 1 Samuel 30. When bad things happen, the enemy is always right there to whisper, "Where is your God now? If He loved you, why would He allow this to happen? He doesn't care about you. Trusting Him is a waste of time."

What was David's response to the taunts of the enemy? "Why are you cast down, O my soul? And why are you disquieted within me? Hope in God; for I shall yet praise Him, the help of my countenance and my God" (Psalm 42:11). David spoke to his own soul—for the second time; he did the same thing in verse 5. He does the same thing in Psalm 43:5, speaking the same encouraging words to his own soul. When you find yourself in distressing circumstances, do whatever you need to do in order to build yourself up.

After a thorough examination and set of X-rays had been done, an acquaintance of mine was told that a spot had been found on his lung that was likely cancerous. He immediately canceled all of his speaking engagements and locked himself in a room in his house with the Bible. For the next several days, all he did was worship while reading and reflecting on God's promises of healing. Finally, after strengthening himself and sensing a clear note of victory in his spirit, he came out of that room and made another doctor's appointment. Upon another battery of tests and fresh X-rays, it was determined that whatever had been in his lung before was gone. That was several decades ago, and to this day he has remained healthy.

## THOUGHT 4: Seek direction.

The next thing David did was to seek direction from God (1 Samuel 30:7–8). In fact, he inquired about two specific things. One dealt with the "what" he should do and the other with the "when" he should do it. "Shall I pursue this troop?" That is the what. "Shall I overtake them?" That deals with the when, for if they could not overtake them before they made it back to their fortified city, another strategy would need to be employed and the pursuit may need to wait.

When seeking direction from God, the "when" may be just as important as the "what." My dad had the most beautiful persimmon tree that you have ever seen, and it may have been the most fruitful as well. Every year it gave so much fruit that the branches needed to be propped up lest they break under the weight. The fruit was always sweet and delicious, unless you tried to eat one before it was ripe. Anyone that has ever taken a bite out of a green persimmon knows what I am talking about. They are so astringent that your mouth seems to turn into sandpaper.

In the same way, something that is in the plan of God for your life partaken of too early can be bitter and disappointing. Ecclesiastes 3:1 teaches us, "To everything there is a season, a time for every purpose under heaven." With that in mind, it is important to consider timing when you seek the Lord for direction.

## Called to Pastor

Years ago, while I was staying with some friends, I was earnestly praying about God's will for my future. I had been pacing back and forth in their backyard, quietly praying in the Spirit while occasionally stopping to become quiet and listen. After about an hour of prayer, the Lord spoke to me. He told me that He had called me to be a pastor. That was actually the first time that thought had ever even occurred to me.

From the time I was saved, I had an abiding sense that I was called to gospel ministry, but my thoughts were that I would be a traveling teacher. Up to that time I had never seen a healthy church or a pastor that I wanted to be like, but I had been in the meetings of several traveling teachers and evangelists who had inspired me. They were the only models of successful ministry that I had seen. And now, God was telling me that I was called to pastor a church!

I was wise enough to not immediately go out and try to start a church. Looking back, if I had done so, I would have skinned all the sheep alive and nailed their hides to the church's back wall. To put it mildly, I was a bit on the harsh side in my dealings with people at that stage. Call it "young man's disease" if you like, but to my shame I had an answer for everything back then, and my typical response to people in difficulties was, "Stop whining and start doing the Word!"

As it turned out, it wasn't until after more than four years that Janet and I began Cottonwood Church. And during those interim years, more than anything else, God worked on my character in the areas of compassion and patience. God knew what I needed and His timing was perfect.

In the last chapter, we saw how Moses had the direction right, but he had the method and timing wrong for being Israel's deliverer, and his first attempt turned out to be a bit of a disaster. If we will take the time to inquire, like David, God will guide us in both the "what to do" and the "when to do it." A careful study of David's life will reveal that inquiring of the Lord was a habit of life for him. (See 1 Samuel 23:2–4; 30:8; 2 Samuel 2:1; 5:19, 23; 21:1; 1 Chronicles 14:10, 14.)

### *Expect an Answer*

I love the succinctness of these words from 1 Samuel 30:8: "David inquired of the Lord . . . . and He answered him." That is basically what the story in 1 Samuel 30 tells us. David asked, God answered. When we inquire of the Lord, we should anticipate an answer. Perhaps it may require us to slow down and quiet our hearts before Him long enough to discern what He is saying, **but we must come expectantly.** Even as David says in Psalm 86:7, "In the day of my trouble I will call upon You, for You will answer me."

Years ago, a friend of mine and Janet's was heading down a path that—to us—was obviously wrong. She was a believer, but in the process of following this pathway, she had cut herself off from Christian fellowship and stopped coming to church. In our concern, Janet and I went to visit her. She was pleasant enough, but when the conversation got around to the choices she was making, the mood changed somewhat. "This is what I've decided to do, and I'm going to do it," she matter-of-factly told us. "Have you asked the Lord about it?" I asked her. "No. Absolutely not!" she shot back. "Why?" I asked. "Because He will probably answer me!" she exclaimed.

It's amazing how confident we can be that God will speak to us when it comes to correction and letting us know when we are in the wrong, and at the same time be doubtful that He will guide us when we are in need. If you have experienced the loss of something in your life, don't panic or act rashly. Seek direction from the Lord, expecting Him to answer you and help you in the pursuit of recovery.

## THOUGHT 5: Continue to serve others.

> So David went, he and the six hundred men who were with him, and came to the Brook Besor, where those stayed who were left behind. But David pursued, he and four hundred men; for two hundred stayed behind, who were so weary that they could not cross the Brook Besor. (1 Samuel 30:9–10)

Even in your weariness and fatigue, God may use you to fight for others. Two hundred men remained behind because they were too tired to continue the chase. David would not only have to fight on their behalf, he would have to successfully lead the remaining four hundred men that were—a short time before—speaking of stoning him!

David was just as weary as they were; his loss was just as great as theirs; his grief was on par with theirs; and to make matters worse, he was saddled with the task of leading a group of men that were just on the verge of mutiny and murder! Again, **even when you are at the point of personal weakness and perplexity, God will use you to help others.**

## *A Word for Those in Leadership*

Men and women in roles of leadership especially need to consider what I am saying. Don't expect most people to think about your needs. They will generally only think about their own. You can't get mad at them for not considering that you're going through things as well or that you might be fatigued or weary. David didn't become resentful toward his men; he went the extra mile on their behalf. God will use you to help others when you're weak or facing trials just to remind you that it's Him, not you, leading and sustaining things in the first place.

A friend of mine who used to hold salvation and healing crusades in a huge tent around the country told me this story. He said, "I had preached my heart out that night and had literally laid my hands on thousands of people for healing. When the evening was through, I was utterly exhausted! Emotionally and physically. I didn't have the strength to talk to one more person or to pray for anyone. As I was being ushered to my car, a woman broke through the security men around me and grabbed my pant leg as she fell to the ground. When she got up, she began to scream, 'I'm healed! I'm healed! The Lord just healed me!' I couldn't believe it!" he told me. "I couldn't have felt more drained or more bereft of anything to give. I feel like it was just the Lord reminding me that it was Him and not me doing the work."

Some years back, I had arrived home from a rigorous ministry trip in Australia only to turn around and head to Europe for a series of meetings in different cities. The schedule was tight with a lot of train and plane rides between meetings and not a lot of time for rest. I was already jet lagged, and now that was compounded with the jump through so many time zones. Toward the end of that trip, I was so fatigued that I felt like I could sleep standing up. To make matters worse, I was fighting a cold. It was one of our last scheduled meetings and I couldn't have felt worse. I was like a zombie. Somehow, I preached my message and managed to give a bleary-eyed altar call. Eighty-four people responded and came forward to receive Christ! It was the largest response any of the participating churches had ever seen. To myself I just whispered, "I know Lord, you've been the wind in the sails all along, and this just makes it even clearer."

In 2 Corinthians 12:10, Paul declares, "Therefore I take pleasure in infirmities, in reproaches, in needs, in persecutions, in distresses, for Christ's sake. **For when I am weak, then I am strong**" (emphasis mine). Are you going through troubles right now? Perhaps you're fighting for your health or grappling with family or financial issues. Remember, you can still be used by God to meet the needs of others and to strengthen and encourage them. Continue to serve others, even when you are in need yourself.

# THOUGHT 6: Be open for help to come from unexpected sources.

"Then they found an Egyptian in the field, and brought him to David; and they gave him bread and he ate, and they let him drink water" (1 Samuel 30:11). This Egyptian led David and his men straight to the Amalekite camp. It was a completely unexpected turn of events for he was a servant of one of the raiders who had kidnapped the families of David and his men! Once you have prayed and asked the Lord for His help, don't be too surprised at who He uses to help you in the recovery process. He may even choose to use someone that you might classify as the worst of sinners.

### *Stuck Near Dead Indian Road*

Many years ago, I was traveling between Klamath Falls, Oregon, and the city of Ashland along a stretch called "Dead Indian Road." It was winter and there was a lot of snow on the ground. We decided to explore an unmarked mountain road that intersected the main road. Off we went, slipping this way and that on the narrow, snowy track for several miles until we finally became hopelessly stuck in the snow.

After several hours of trying to free the vehicle, we came to grips with the fact that we were not going to succeed. Walking out was out of the question as it was far too long a journey, and with daylight fading, we were looking at spending the night in temperatures that would plummet below freezing. I didn't know what else to do, so I grabbed my Bible and began reading. I came upon Psalm 107, which I read over and over. Among other things, it gave instance after instance where God rescued people out of their troubles. I still remember putting my head on the steering wheel and praying, "God, you did it for them, do it for us. Send help."

I realized how unlikely an answer to that prayer was. We were on an isolated—what would have been dirt had it not been covered with snow—road, late in the evening, but I felt confident in my heart that God had heard me. About thirty minutes later, we heard voices. It was a four-wheel drive coming down the track with four drunks in it. It's good they were driving because they were too drunk to walk. They stopped, hooked a chain to our vehicle, and pulled us out.

The driver proceeded to tell me that they didn't even know why they had turned down that road. I will never forget the look on his face when I told him that I had prayed and that God had sent them as an answer to my prayer. He couldn't have been more stunned if I had hit him in the face with a wet mackerel. Sometimes God sends help from unexpected sources!

### *Kill the Egyptian*

Some in David's party would have said, "Kill the Egyptian! God has judged him for his part in the raid by delivering him into our hands." But David showed him kindness—and God rewarded that choice. We are told in Romans 12:20, "If your enemy is hungry, feed him; if he is thirsty, give him a drink; for in so doing you will heap coals of fire on his head." Some of the greatest antagonists of the gospel have been won to Christ through love and kindness.

When we were in the throes of our legal battles over our church property, God sent help and encouragement from many unexpected sources. Some came from Christians and some came from people that many in the church would have branded as sinners and "enemies of the gospel." We were just thankful that the help came. In fact, some of our greatest help and encouragement came at critical times from unsaved people, some of whom we have not met to this day.

You never know who you might need or who God might use in your life, so as long as you're not required to compromise your convictions, it's a good policy to not burn down any existing bridges between yourself and others. God will use the saved and unsaved, the sanctified and the unsanctified to fulfill His will and to help His children when they are in need.

Our God is a God of recovery and restoration, but as with so many other things it is not automatic. David sought God about recovery before it happened. As we proactively seek God concerning the pursuit of lost things, I believe that we will find Him to be a very present help in times of trouble (Psalm 46:1).

## A PLAN FOR PURSUIT

He restores my soul; He leads me in the paths of righteousness for His name's sake.

Psalm 23:3

Thoughts, prayers, and questions to help you make a plan for pursuing lost things.

- ▶ The heart of God toward you is that of a good shepherd. And that is the first thing the enemy attacks when you suffer loss. Because if he can get you to doubt God's goodness, then he can keep you from God's peace, purpose, and restoration. Take some time now to prayerfully affirm that God is for you, sees you, loves you, and is with you, even in your loss.

- ▶ Consider this: We do not have a God who has never suffered, but one who suffered on your behalf. He knows pain and heartache, and even though it endures for a time, He will one day wipe away every tear (Revelation 21:4).

- ▶ Can you think of a loss that God has brought you through? What lessons did you learn on the journey? How has your experience changed the way you treat others when they suffer loss or heartache?

- We learned in this chapter that God is a God of recovery and restoration. How can you bear witness to that truth in your own life? How can you invite others to experience God's restoration for themselves?

# POSTSCRIPT

Well, you have finished the book. Perhaps one chapter or one point in a chapter reached out and grabbed you. Maybe a lot of things resonated with you. That's good. But it won't help you in the long run if you don't do something with what you have learned or with what God has whispered to your heart through these pages. My prayer is that you will be an active participant and not merely a spectator in the great pursuits outlined in this book.

Yours in Christ,

Bayless

WWW.BAYLESSCONLEY.TV